Overcoming Evil in Prison

How to Be a Light in a Dark Place

Steven R. Cook, M. Div.

Overcoming Evil in Prison: How to Be a Light in a Dark Place

© 2012 by Steven R. Cook, (M. Div.)

Steven R. Cook earned a Master of Divinity from Southwestern Baptist Theological Seminary.

This book is dedicated to those Christians in jail or prison who are serving the Lord Jesus Christ in their environment and proving to be a light in a dark place.

TABLE OF CONTENTS

Overcoming Evil in Prison

Overcoming Evil in Prison

Preface

I trusted Christ for salvation when I was young boy, but after years away from the church, I began to live like the world around me, and seven years of heavy drug use eventuated in my living on the streets of Las Vegas, Nevada. I lived on the streets for a short time and then stayed at a Salvation Army homeless shelter for a few weeks. The summer of 1988 was a rough period in my life. After running from my probation officer for several months, I decided to turn myself in and face my drug charges. As a Christian, I decided to take responsibility for my life and accept whatever punishment I deserved, and I certainly deserved more than I got.

I'd been in the County Jail several times before; however, rather than try to manipulate my release by calling family and friends like I'd done in the past, I decided to put my trust in God alone and live by faith in Him. I wanted God and His will for my life more than I wanted my freedom. I made phone calls and wrote letters, but was very careful not to slip into my old practice of trying to manipulate others to gain my liberty. Old habits die hard, but I knew if I was going to make it as a Christian, I had to start living like one, which meant living by faith in God's Word. Obedience to Scripture was necessary, though it was not always easy. My resolve to live as a Christian was soon tested.

While in jail, I knew the possibility of going to prison was real, and I prayed to the Lord to spare me that trip. But unlike the times before, I decided that if I did go to prison that I would accept it as the Lord's will for my life and I would thank Him for His love and would strive to serve Him in whatever environment I found myself. On February 9, 1989, my probation was revoked and I was sentenced to two years in prison. I went back to my cell and got on my knees and thanked God for His will in my life. Thanking God that morning was difficult, but it was the biblical thing to do (1 Thess. 5:18). I served my prison term as an active Christian. I read my Bible daily, shared the gospel many times, prayed often, and encouraged other Christians in their spiritual walk whenever I had an opportunity to do so. Like many other Christians, I faced pressure to conform to the evil that surrounded me, but the Lord's grace sustained me and I was able to advance spiritually and be a light in a dark place.

Four months after my release from prison I started serving in jail ministry and continued for over twelve years. I loved teaching Bible classes several times a week

4

and sharing the gospel with inmates who would listen. I also started college and was able to complete a Bachelor of Science degree in Human Services and then went to graduate school where I earned a Master of Divinity degree from Southwestern Baptist Theological Seminary in Fort Worth, Texas. On February 10, 2005, I was awarded a full pardon by the Governor of Nevada for the crime that sent me to prison and one year later had my records sealed. This too was the grace of God in my life.

Now I find myself in a place of simple ministry, teaching God's Word in home Bible studies and to a very small church on a weekly basis. I even find time to write. I still face the pressures of evil around me, and God who sustained me in prison continues to sustain me as I live by faith in Him. God's grace has become central to my life; for it was by grace that I was saved, and it is by grace that I live every moment in this world.

Overcoming Evil in Prison

Introduction

For the average inmate, prison is a place where his volition is restrained mainly because he failed to adjust and live by the judicial laws that govern American society. There's even a special place in prison known as solitary confinement for those inmates who refuse to adjust and live by the laws that govern the prison. Groups of inmates create their own laws and expect other inmates to live by them and failure to understand those laws can cause serious problems for someone trying to fit in. Everyone lives by laws, but not all laws are equal, and not all laws are good. The laws created by inmates are also policed and judged by them; but such laws are usually self serving and spring from sinful motives which demean others and never glorify God.

A lot of evil things happen in prison, but prison is not an evil place. Prison is no better or worse than the people who make up its population. Evil refers both to the attitudes and actions of people who conform to Satan's value system. Prisons are usually full of people given over to unrestrained evil motives. Though a government cannot change a person's attitude, it can restrain his behavior by imprisoning him. A prison, properly used by a government, prevents a criminal from 1) causing harm to law abiding citizens and, 2) disrupting the basic harmony necessary to a well-functioning society. Bad choices in society can result in the loss freedom. Bad choices in prison to conform to evil only perpetuate the loss of freedom and make the environment a difficult place to live.

A prison, like any social environment, is no better or worse than those people who live in it. People create society, and prison is a micro-society made up of persons who contribute either to its beauty or ugliness. A prison could reflect the highest and best in human behavior, if the people living in the prison are Christians committed to serving God and each other with an attitude of humility and love. Sadly, the majority of those living in prison reflect the lowest and worst in humanity because they are governed by their sin nature and their thinking is rooted in worldliness and selfishness. The Christian who lives in prison feels the pressure of evil all around him by those who want him to conform to their values. The Christian is not alone, as God and the light of His Word penetrate even the darkest places of this world. There is no place the Christian can go to escape His presence and power (Ps. 139). This book is written to the Christian who is living in prison. It is written to the Christian who wants to walk with God and not conform to the pressures of his environment. The challenges of the Christian living in prison can be daunting, but God always equips His child with the necessary resources to know and walk in the light of His truth. This book is designed to educate and encourage Christians to be a light in a dark place.

Overcoming Evil in Prison

Chapter 1

Getting Right with God

The Bible teaches that God is holy, which means He is absolutely righteous in essence and action. The word *holy* (Hebrew *qadosh* and Greek *hagios*) means sacred from all that is sinful or set apart from all that is common (Lev. 11:44-45; Josh. 24:19; Ps. 99:9; Isa. 6:3; John 17:11; 1 Pet. 1:14-16; Rev. 15:4). Scripture declares "that God is Light, and in Him there is no darkness at all" (1 John 1:5), and *"Your* eyes are too pure to approve evil, and You can not look on wickedness *with favor"* (Hab. 1:13). Sin is identified as that which does not conform to the holy character of God. However, being holy is not merely the absence of sin or defilement, but also the presence of that which is righteous and good. God is positively righteous in essence and action and this completely sets Him apart from all that is sinful. "Holiness is one of the most important, if not the most important, attributes of God, and certainly nothing that God does can be done apart from being in complete harmony with His holy nature."[1]

---

[1] Charles C. Ryrie, *A Survey of Bible Doctrine* (Chicago: Moody Press, 1995), 19.

God's holiness means His complete "apartness" from anything that is sinful. He is *different* from that which is common; He is *separate* from that which is defiling. But God's holiness isn't a static thing, like a block of pure ice. His holiness is active and alive, a "sea of glass mingled with fire" (Rev. 15:2). Everything about God is holy: His wisdom, His power, His judgments, and even His love. If His love were not a holy love, He would never have sent His only Son to die for the sins of the world and meet the just demands of His own nature and His own holy law.[2]

Too often people come to God as though He were a big fluffy teddy bear waiting to be squeezed, or a kindly old man who poses no threat to anyone. God never portrays Himself this way in Scripture, as though He were soft and easy. Men who see God's holiness stand in awe of Him and have respect for His greatness. More so, because God is holy He must stay separate from sinners, and those who encounter God's holiness are afraid for their lives. Moses was not allowed to approach the Lord when he met Him at the burning bush; rather, the Lord said "do not come near here; remove your sandals from your feet,

---

[2] Warren Wiersbe, *The Bible Exposition Commentary: Old Testament*, Vol. 1 (Colorado Springs, Col., Victor Books, 2001), 306.

for the place on which you are standing is holy ground" (Ex. 3:5). Later, when God revealed Himself to the Israelites at Mount Sinai, "the people perceived the thunder and the lightning flashes and the sound of the trumpet and the mountain smoking" (Ex. 20:18a). Rather than run to God as One to be embraced as a cuddly friend, "they trembled and stood at a distance" (Ex. 20:18b). The prophet Isaiah once encountered God in His holiness and the event disturbed Him greatly.

> In the year of King Uzziah's death I saw the Lord sitting on a throne, lofty and exalted, with the train of His robe filling the temple. Seraphim stood above Him, each having six wings: with two he covered his face, and with two he covered his feet, and with two he flew. And one called out to another and said, "Holy, Holy, Holy, is the LORD of hosts, The whole earth is full of His glory." And the foundations of the thresholds trembled at the voice of him who called out, while the temple was filling with smoke. (Isa. 6:1-4)

After seeing the holiness of God, Isaiah declared "Woe is me, for I am ruined! Because I am a man of unclean lips, and I live among a people of unclean lips; for my eyes have seen the King, the LORD of hosts" (Isa.

6:5). Isaiah thought he was about to die, because He knew
he was a sinner standing in the presence of the absolute
holy and righteous God. When the Apostle John saw the
risen Jesus Christ in His glory and majesty he "fell at His
feet like a dead man" (Rev. 1:17). To know God properly
is to know that He is holy. To know the holiness of God is
to have respect and reverence for Him, for "who will not
fear, O Lord, and glorify Your name? For You alone are
holy" (Rev. 15:4).

It is only in the light of God's holiness that men
realize they are not in right relationship with Him. "As it
is written 'there is none righteous, not even one'…for all
have sinned and fall short of the glory of God" (Rom. 3:10,
23). By God's estimation all men are fallen in sin. Being
fallen in sin does not mean that men are as sinful as they
can be, or that they engage in every form of sinful
behavior, but that sin permeates and contaminates every
aspect of their being and lives. Men are sinners at the very
core of their being, and this leads them to be sinners in
their thoughts and actions. Men are sinners in three ways:

1. By imputation of Adam's sin (Rom. 5:12-14).
2. By nature (Ps. 51:5; Rom. 7:19-21; Eph. 2:3).
3. By choice (1 Kings 8:46; Rom. 3:9-18).

Biblically, there is both a moral and immoral side to sin. When most people hear the word *sin*, they think of immoral acts (murder, rape, lying, stealing, etc.). However, there is a moral side to sin that often takes a religious form in which men seek to establish a self-righteous code of ethics by which they think God will accept them and other people will hold them in high regard (Matt. 23:1-8). Jesus dealt with such people in His day (Pharisees and Sadducees), and it was this group of sinners that crucified Him because He jeopardized their place of importance in society by exposing their hypocrisy and threatening their place of religious power (Matt. 23:13-36; John 11:47-48).

Moral sinners often create religions in an effort to adjust themselves to God. They think that if they follow the right set of rules or live by a certain set of ethics that God will smile on them and accept them into heaven. However, our best efforts are sinful when they bypass or seek to modify God's solution of the cross.

> For all of us have become like one who is unclean, and all our righteous deeds are like a filthy garment; and all of us wither like a leaf, and our iniquities, like the wind, take us away. (Isa. 64:6)

15

For not knowing about God's righteousness and seeking to establish their own, they did not subject themselves to the righteousness of God; for Christ is the end of the law for righteousness to everyone who believes. (Rom. 10:3-4)

For the word of the cross is foolishness to those who are perishing, but to us who are being saved it is the power of God. (1 Cor. 1:18)

Arrogant men bring their good works to God and expect Him to fling open the gates of heaven and welcome them. Hell will be full of these kinds of people. God accepts only the substitutionary atoning work of His Son on the cross, because there is no system of law or good works men can follow to save themselves; for "if a law had been given which was able to impart life, then righteousness would indeed have been based on law" (Gal. 3:21). Jesus' death on the cross is the only act that satisfies God's righteous demands toward our sin (Rom. 3:25; 1 Jo. 2:2; 4:10). There is no salvation without the cross of Christ. May we all say with the Apostle Paul, "may it never be that I would boast, except in the cross of our Lord Jesus Christ" (Gal. 6:14).

As stated previously, we are sinners *by nature* (Ps.

16

51:5; Rom. 7:19-21; Eph. 2:3), *by choice* (1 Kings 8:46; Rom. 3:9-18), and *by imputation of Adam's sin* (Rom. 5:12-14). Our *sin nature* is that indispensable part of our being that draws us toward things that are sinful and is perpetually hostile to God and His will (Gal. 5:17). The sin nature is indispensable in that it is part of who we are from birth and it will not be removed from us until death. *We are sinners by choice* when we manufacture sin from the source of our volition and say yes to temptation. We can be tempted internally from the source of our sin nature, or externally from the world. Temptation is not sin, but is the opportunity to sin. Jesus was "tempted in all things as *we are, yet* without sin" (Heb. 4:15; cf. Matt. 4:1-11). Lastly, *we are sinners in Adam*, because we are identified with him when he died spiritually in the Garden of Eden. When it comes to our being condemned before God, it was the one sin that Adam committed in the Garden of Eden that is the greatest sin of all! Adam was created perfect and without sin, yet willfully committed rebellion against God when he ate the forbidden fruit of "the tree of the knowledge of good and evil" (Gen. 2:16-17). Adam knowingly "took from its fruit and ate" and brought spiritual and physical death to himself as well as to all his descendants who were born after him (Gen. 3:6). Scripture tells us:

When Adam had lived one hundred and thirty years, he became the father of *a son* in his own [sinful]³ likeness, according to his [fallen] image, and named him Seth. (Genesis 5:3)

Adam's sons were sinners. Cain and Abel both had to bring sacrifices to God to satisfy His holiness, and this was because they were sinners in need of atonement. After the fall of Adam the human race grew in great numbers, but "the LORD saw that the wickedness of man was great on the earth, and that every intent of the thoughts of his heart was only evil continually" (Gen. 6:5). Sinful men give birth to sinful men, and this goes all the way back to Adam, the first man. The Apostle Paul points out that all men are sinners in Adam when he writes:

Therefore, just as through one man [the first man, Adam] sin entered into the world, and death through sin, and so death [spiritual and physical] spread to all men, because all sinned [when Adam sinned]. (Rom. 5:12)

For since by a man [Adam] came death, by a man [Jesus] also came the resurrection of the dead. For

---

³ All bracketed words or comments found in NASB quotations are mine and are added for clarification of the biblical text.

as in Adam all die, so also in Christ all [who believe in Him] will be made alive. (1 Cor. 15:21-22)

According to the Apostle Paul, all humanity died spiritually and is subject to physical death because of the one sin of Adam. Even newborn babies die physically, though not because of any sin they personally commit since they are too young to produce sin of their own.[4] Babies die because of the sin Adam committed in the Garden of Eden, and this is what Paul means when he writes "through one man sin entered into the world, and death through sin, and so death spread to all men" (Rom. 5:12).

> Because Adam had the sentence of death imposed as an actual operational feature of his biological life, his descendants also have inherited a life principle which involves a built-in death principle. The moment a child is conceived he begins to die, and eventually the death principle wins out over the life principle and he does die. As the tendency toward death is inherited by all men, so also is the tendency

---

[4] Babies who die before the age of God consciousness automatically go to heaven since they are too young to understand God's grace-provision of salvation through the cross of Christ. The book *Safe in the Arms of Jesus* by Dr. Robert Lightner is an excellent resource that best explains baby-theology.

toward sin. No descendant of Adam has ever lived to an age of conscious awareness of right and wrong without actually *choosing* wrong. He has become a deliberate sinner because he has inherited a sinful nature, which leads him to sin in practice. Thus, "death passed upon all men, for that *all have sinned.*" Each person continues under the divine judgment of death, not only because of Adam's sin, but because of his own deliberate sin.[5]

Condemnation *in Adam* is sometimes a challenge for people to accept because they often say it's not fair. Why should they be condemned because of another man's actions? Really, one could argue on the same grounds that God was unfair to send His innocent Son to die on the cross and bear the wrath that rightfully belongs to sinners. Biblically, God cannot be accused of unfairness because He has provided a way for men to be saved through the substitutionary atoning death of Christ. Adam freely sinned and brought death upon the human race, and Christ freely went to the cross and obeyed the will of His father and provided salvation for all who will trust Him as Savior. Death comes automatically to all who are born in Adam,

---

[5] Henry M. Morris, *The Genesis Record: A Scientific and Devotional Commentary on the Book of Beginnings* (Grand Rapids, MI: Baker Books, 1976), 113.

and life comes to those who by faith trust in Christ as their Savior.

In his letter to the Christians at Ephesus, Paul painted a very dark picture about their life prior to salvation in Christ. Paul was forthright in his choice of words and never sought to soften the truth, especially when it came to the subject of sin. Paul stated:

> And you [Christians at Ephesus] were [before salvation] dead in your trespasses and sins, in which you formerly walked according to the course [patterned values] of this world, according to the prince of the power of the air [Satan], of the spirit that is now working in the sons of disobedience [rebellious unbelievers]. Among them we too all formerly lived [before being saved] in the lusts of our flesh, indulging the desires of the flesh and of the mind, and were by nature children of wrath [enemies of God], even as the rest [of humanity]. (Eph. 2:1-3)

When men are without Christ, they are physically alive but spiritually dead. Being spiritually dead means no spiritual life! It means no capacity for understanding or appreciating things that God has revealed about Himself in

Scripture.   More so, on the negative side, it means the unbeliever has a natural affinity for things satanic and that he is drawn to the manmade institutions of this world which are in many ways hostile to God.

> In the Bible, *death* basically means "separation," not only physically, as the spirit separated from the body (James 2:26), but also spiritually, as the spirit separated from God (Isa. 59:2). The unbeliever is not sick; he is dead! He does not need resuscitation; he needs resurrection. All lost sinners are dead, and the only difference between one sinner and another is the state of decay. The lost derelict on skid row may be more decayed outwardly than the unsaved society leader, but both are dead in sin—and one corpse cannot be more dead than another! This means that our world is one vast graveyard, filled with people who are dead while they live (1 Tim. 5:6).[6]

God is holy, and men are sinners who cannot save themselves.   The biblical teaching is that helpless sinners must be rescued from their helpless situation.   God must come to them with His gospel and "open their eyes so that

---

[6] Warren Wiersbe, *The Bible Exposition Commentary: New Testament*, Vol. 2, 17-18.

they may turn from darkness to light and from the dominion of Satan to God" (Acts 26:18). Such grace on behalf of God is a display of His wonderful mercy toward them. Paul, who wrote about the terrible condition of the Christians at Ephesus prior to their being born again, also described their salvation as an act of God's mercy.

> But God, being rich in mercy, because of His great love with which He loved us, even when we were [spiritually] dead in our transgressions, made us [spiritually] alive together with Christ (by grace you have been saved), and raised us up with Him, and seated us with Him in the heavenly *places* in Christ Jesus, so that in the ages to come He might show the surpassing riches of His grace in kindness toward us in Christ Jesus. (Ephesians 2:4-7)

Here is God's grace in action! Prior to salvation, the Christians at Ephesus were living in the trash heap of sin, wallowing in a state of spiritual death and headed toward the trash heap of eternity known as the Lake of Fire. Yet God, "being rich in mercy, because of His great love" reached down into their trash heap lives and gave them spiritual life at the moment they trusted Christ as their Savior and raised them up and seated them "with Him in the heavenly *places* in Christ Jesus" (Eph. 2:6).

Over against the dark picture of human ruin presented in Ephesians 2:1-3, the Apostle now proceeds...to set forth the only existing hope for man, namely, the fact that God is "rich in mercy for his great love wherewith he loved us, even when we were dead in sins." With full recognition of the depths to which man has fallen, it is nevertheless declared that there is abundant salvation for all who *believe:* a salvation which so far exceeds the ruin that it not only reverses all that man lost by the fall, but it lifts him up far above his original unfallen state to the highest conceivable position in heaven, there to share forever the fellowship and the glory of the Triune God.[7]

God took these people from a place of darkness and brought them into a place of light. He took them from death to life and raised them to the very heights of heaven so that their new life would forever be identified with Christ where He is, now seated at the right hand of the Father. We share that same life and position in Christ at the moment we trust Jesus as our Savior. At the moment of salvation we can say with the Apostle Paul that God

---

[7] Lewis S. Chafer, *The Epistle to the Ephesians* (Grand Rapids, MI., Kregel Publications, 1991), 63.

"rescued us from the domain of darkness, and transferred us to the kingdom of His beloved Son, in whom we have redemption, the forgiveness of sins" (Col. 1:13-14). What's amazing is that God revealed His love toward us while we were sinners and living in rebellion to Him.

> For while we were still helpless, at the right time Christ died for the ungodly. For one will hardly die for a righteous man; though perhaps for the good man someone would dare even to die. But God demonstrates His own love toward us, in that while we were yet sinners, Christ died for us. Much more then, having now been justified by His blood, we shall be saved from the wrath *of God* through Him. For if while we were enemies we were reconciled to God through the death of His Son, much more, having been reconciled, we shall be saved by His life. (Rom. 5:6-10)

God revealed His love toward us while were *helpless*, *ungodly*, *sinners*, and *enemies* who were hostile to Him. The Bible never paints a flattering picture of men, but rather casts them in an honest light and portrays them as helpless sinners in need of God's grace. Men do nothing to save themselves, whereas God does everything, and God alone gets the glory. That's the way it should be!

When you were dead in your transgressions and the uncircumcision of your flesh [before being saved], He [God the Father] made you alive together with Him [Jesus], having forgiven us all our transgressions, having canceled out the certificate of debt consisting of decrees against us, which was hostile to us; and He has taken it out of the way, having nailed it to the cross (Col. 2:13-14).

The gospel is the solution to the problem of sin. It is the good news "that Christ died for our sins according to the Scriptures, and that He was buried, and that He was raised on the third day according to the Scriptures" (1 Cor. 15:3-4). A person is saved when He accepts this good news and trusts Christ as his Savior. Salvation is a free gift to sinners who do not deserve it. It is free to the sinner, though it cost God the death of His dear Son who died on the cross in the sinner's place. Peter tells us that Jesus died for our sins, "*the* just for *the* unjust, so that He might bring us to God" (1 Pet. 3:18). If a sinner got what he deserved, he'd burn forever in the Lake of Fire (Rev. 20:15). God, by His wonderful grace, treats us better than we deserve.

For by grace you have been saved through faith; and that not of yourselves, it is the gift of God; not as a result of works, so that no one may boast. (Eph. 2:8-9)

He saved us, not on the basis of deeds which we have done in righteousness, but according to His mercy, by the washing of regeneration and renewing by the Holy Spirit. (Titus 3:5)

Good works never save. It is the work of Christ alone that provides salvation to sinners. It's not a matter of giving men what they deserve, but treating them better than they deserve, which is what grace is all about. "For by grace you have been saved through faith" are perhaps the sweetest words a sinner can hear at the moment he turns to Christ as His Savior. We come with the empty hands of faith, not trusting in ourselves at all, but casting ourselves completely on the finished work of Christ who completely bore God's wrath in our place on the cross. Even a mute quadriplegic who cannot speak or ever perform one kind deed can be forever saved if he trusts in Christ for salvation.

Throughout his entire life, the Christian is to continue in the truth that he is saved by grace alone through faith alone in Christ alone. Good works are the expected fruit of the saved life, but they are never the condition of it. Men are saved to perform good deeds, but good deeds never save anyone, nor do they keep men saved. Paul made this very clear when he wrote to Christians at Philippi:

> But whatever things were gain to me [good works according to the Mosaic Law], those things I have counted as loss for the sake of Christ. More than that, I count all things to be loss in view of the surpassing value of knowing Christ Jesus my Lord, for whom I have suffered the loss of all things, and count them but rubbish [Grk. *skubalon* – lit. dung] so that I may gain Christ, and may be found in Him, not having a righteousness of my own derived from the Law, but that which is through faith in Christ, the [imputed gift of] righteousness which comes from God on the basis of faith. (Phil. 3:7-9)

Men are saved and declared righteous before God at the moment they place their faith in Jesus Christ as their savior. At the moment of faith in Christ, God gives them His righteousness as a gift. This gifting of divine righteousness is called *imputation*. The sinner is declared righteous at the moment he trusts Christ for salvation and is forever justified in God's sight.

Justification is a divine act whereby an infinitely Holy God judicially declares a believing sinner to be righteous and acceptable before Him because Christ has borne the sinner's sin on the cross and has become "to us...righteousness" (1 Cor. 1:30; Rom. 3:24). Justification springs from the fountain of God's grace (Titus 3:4-5). It is operative as the result of the redemptive and propitiatory sacrifice of Christ, who has settled all the claims of the law (Rom. 3:24-25; 5:9). Justification is on the basis of faith and not by human merit or works (3:28-30; 4:5; Gal. 2:16). In this marvelous operation of God the infinitely holy Judge judicially declares righteous the one who believes in Jesus (Rom. 8:31-34).[8]

Like the Apostle Paul, every Christian should desire to "be found in Him, not having a righteousness of my own derived from the Law, but that which is through faith in Christ, the [imputed gift of] righteousness which comes from God on the basis of faith" (Phil. 3:9). Once we trust in Christ for salvation, we are at that very moment made right with God, and can begin the process of developing our spiritual life wherever we are. By this God is glorified.

---

[8] Merrill F. Unger, "Justification" *The New Unger's Bible Dictionary* (Chicago: Moody Press, 1988), 729.

After we come into a right relationship with God by trusting in Christ as our Savior, we can then "draw near with confidence to the throne of grace, so that we may receive mercy and find grace to help in time of need" (Heb. 4:16). God sits both on a throne of judgment as well as a throne of grace. How we respond to God's free-grace offer of eternal life by faith in Jesus Christ determines which throne we will stand before. God poured out His wrath on Jesus when He died on the cross as a substitute for sinners (Rom. 5:6-10; 1 Cor. 15:3-4). Jesus died a death He did not deserve and bore the punishment that rightfully belongs to sinners. Scripture states "Christ also died for sins once for all, *the* just for *the* unjust, so that He might bring us to God" (1 Pet. 3:18). Having satisfied every requirement of God's holy demands toward sin, God is free to treat the worst sinner in grace and offer eternal life to those who accept salvation by faith alone in Christ alone.

> For God so loved the world, that He gave His only begotten Son, that whoever believes in Him shall not perish, but have eternal life. (John 3:16)

Overcoming Evil in Prison

Overcoming Evil in Prison

Chapter 2

*O*vercoming Evil

> Do not be overcome by evil, but overcome evil with
> good. (Rom. 12:21)

Evil refers to the sinful attitudes and actions of those who adhere to Satan's values and promote his agenda. Evil actions reveal an evil heart, for "out of the heart come evil thoughts, murders, adulteries, fornications, thefts, false witness, [and] slanders" (Matt. 15:19). Men behave in an evil way because their hearts are corrupt and prone to evil. It was not too long after the fall of Adam and Eve that "the LORD saw that the wickedness of man was great on the earth, and that every intent of the thoughts of his heart was only evil continually" (Gen. 6:5). The Scripture reveals that the heart of every man is bent toward evil, and that "the heart is more deceitful than all else and is desperately sick; who can understand it?" (Jer. 17:9a).

Evil can be moral or immoral, and in either case it is the product of willful creatures who oppose God and His will. Moral evil is seen in many people, but is observed most often in the religious person who does good works that he may be noticed and praised by men (Matt. 6:1-5). The unbelieving Pharisees and Sadducees in Jesus' day are good examples of moral evil. Jesus plainly acknowledged that they were very religious and could be observed in public places praying and giving their money to support their religious agendas (Matt. 6:1-5; Luke 18:9-14); however, Jesus also revealed they were dead inside (Matt. 23:27), and had only the appearance of righteousness (Matt. 23:28). Those possessed with religious arrogance "trusted in themselves that they were righteous, and viewed others with contempt" (Luke 18:9). It was these people that Christ declared "you are of *your* father the devil, and you want to do the desires of your father" (John 8:44). The Pharisees and Sadducees were very religious; but their religious values and practices were in disagreement with God and His Word and this brought them into direct opposition with the Son of God. When Jesus confronted and opposed their evil religious system, they chose to crucify Him rather than change their minds and practices. They paid a terrible price for rejecting the Son of God (Matt. 23:37-38).

> The world does not persecute "religious people,"
> but it does persecute righteous people. Why Cain
> killed Abel is explained in 1 John 3:12: "Because

his own works were evil, and his brother's righteous." The Pharisees and Jewish leaders were religious people, yet they crucified Christ and persecuted the early church.[1]

Moral evil, which is at the base of all self-righteous religious systems, is more dangerous than immoral evil because it has the appearance of respectability and is often praised by the majority in society. Moral evil should not surprise us, "for even Satan disguises himself as an angel of light. Therefore it is not surprising if his servants also disguise themselves as servants of righteousness, whose end will be according to their deeds" (2 Cor. 11:14-15). Theological cults such as Mormonism and Jehovah's Witnesses find inroads into many of today's prisons and are often praised for their moral teachings, though they deny the eternal Sonship of Jesus Christ and hold to a false teaching of salvation by human works. The morally arrogant person seeks to earn salvation by good works; but this is wrong, as salvation is completely by God's grace (Eph. 2:8-9; Gal. 2:16; Tit. 3:5).

Immoral evil is usually condemned by society because it tends to be more destructive. Immoral evil

---

[1] Warren Wiersbe, *The Bible Exposition Commentary: New Testament*, Vol. 2 (Colorado Springs, Col., Victor Books, 2001), 424.

consists of "evil thoughts, fornications, thefts, murders, adulteries, deeds of coveting *and* wickedness, *as well as* deceit, sensuality, envy, slander, pride *and* foolishness" (Mark 7:21-22; cf. Gal. 5:19-21). Today's prisons are filled primarily with people given to immoral evil. To be clear, evil in every form is not acceptable to God and will send a person to the Lake of Fire; however, in Satan's world system, moral evil is more socially acceptable and often praised by governmental leaders because it helps to promote their agendas.

In order for the Christian to overcome evil in every form, he must grow spiritually and live in regular dependence on God the Holy Spirit to sustain and direct his life according to Scripture. The Holy Spirit will never lead the Christian independently of Scripture. Learning God's Word necessarily precedes living His will, as the Christian cannot live what he does not know. Change his mind and you'll change his ways. After regeneration, the Christian's mind is still filled with a lifetime of worldly thinking, which will cause him problems to the degree that it remains the basis for his decisions in life. If he thinks like the world then he'll live like the world. Worldly viewpoint should give way to the light of God's Word as the Christian begins to adjust his thinking and bring it into conformity with the mind of God. As Christians, we are always in the process of "destroying speculations and every lofty thing raised up against the knowledge of God, and *we are* taking every thought captive to the obedience of Christ" (2 Cor. 10:5). We do this so we will "not be conformed to this world, but be transformed by the renewing of your mind, so that you may prove what the will of God is, that which is good and acceptable and perfect" (Rom. 12:2). For the Christian, overcoming evil starts with a change in his thinking that leads to a change in his behavior. Without solid thinking rooted in Scripture, the Christian will not be able to stand against the evil pressures Satan will put on him.

The Christian, whether saved before or after he got to prison, will face tremendous pressure to conform to the values and behaviors of those around him. Not only does the Christian face the external pressure of those who are weak and have given themselves over to Satan's evil system, but he also faces the pressure of his own sin nature that has a natural affinity with the devil's world. If Satan were a broadcaster sending out his radio signal, the sin nature would be that internal receiver that is automatically tuned to its message. There is a part of us that is corrupt and is naturally bent toward evil, whether moral or immoral, and we must be aware of this flaw within ourselves. We are given a new spiritual nature at the moment of salvation, which is naturally tuned to God's message and is receptive to the Holy Spirit. The Christian's new spiritual nature is continually in conflict with his old sinful nature, as these are in complete opposition to each other. The Apostle Paul tells us "the flesh sets its desire against the Spirit, and the Spirit against the flesh; for these are in opposition to one another, so that you may not do the things that you please" (Gal. 5:17; cf. Rom. 8:5-8).

> The old nature (which has its origin in our physical birth) fights against the new nature which we receive when we are born again (Gal. 5:16–26). No amount of self-discipline, no set of man-made rules and regulations, can control this old nature. Only the Holy Spirit of God can enable us to "put to death" the old nature (Rom. 8:12–13) and produce the Spirit's fruit (Gal. 5:22–23) in us through the new nature.[2]

Those in the world who have given themselves over to Satan's evil system often demand that others in their periphery conform to their values. Persecution often comes in stages and is defined as "the suffering or

---

[2] Warren Wiersbe, *The Bible Exposition Commentary, New Testament,* Vol. 2, 480.

pressure, mental, moral, or physical, which authorities, individuals, or crowds inflict on others, especially for opinions or beliefs, with a view to their subjection by recantation, silencing, or, as a last resort, execution."[3] Evil men often employ pressure tactics of all sorts, including violence, in order to obtain their objective. In fact, it was during a time of great persecution by the Roman government that the apostle Paul wrote to Christians and told them they must "not be overcome by evil, but overcome evil with good" (Rom. 12:21). Satan was trying to destroy the early church and many in the Roman government were used by him to persecute Christians. Many Roman officials demanded that Christians recognize Caesar as a god to be worshipped, and if those Christians refused, then they would be persecuted and put to death. The Roman government did not separate state from religion, and if a Roman citizen refused to worship as the state mandated, that citizen would then be guilty of treason and could face capital punishment. Many Christians living in Rome faced persecution because they refused to worship Caesar as a god, and the result was often torture and death.

---

[3] Geoffrey W. Bromily, "Persecution," *International Standard Bible Encyclopedia*, Vol. 3 (Michigan: Eerdmans Publishing Company, 1986), 771.

Overcoming Evil in Prison

The persecution of Christians became heightened in the summer of A.D. 64 when the emperor Nero falsely blamed them for a fire that had burned much of the city of Rome. The false charge unleashed the anger of many hostile citizens, and the fury of Rome exploded against the early church and many Christians died a horrible death. Later, the emperor Domitian (ca. A.D. 81-96) carried out attacks against Christians and persecuted them as well. Herbert W. Workman writes:

Some, suffering the punishment of parricides, were shut up in a sack with snakes and thrown into the sea; others were tied to huge stones and cast into a river. For Christians the cross itself was not deemed sufficient agony; hanging on the tree, they were beaten with rods until their bowels gushed out, while vinegar and salt were rubbed into their wounds. ...Christians were tied to catapults, and so wrenched from limb to limb. Some...were thrown to the beasts; others were tied to their horns. Women were stripped, enclosed in nets, and exposed to the attacks of furious bulls. Many were made to lie on sharp shells, and tortured with scrapers, claws, and pincers, before being delivered to the mercy of the flames. Not a few were broken on the wheel, or torn in pieces by wild horses. Of some the feet were slowly burned away, cold water being dowsed over them the while lest the victims should expire too rapidly. ...Down the backs of others melted lead, hissing and bubbling, was poured; while a few 'by the clemency of the emperor' escaped with the searing out of their eyes, or the tearing off of their legs.[4]

To avoid such persecutions by Roman governmental officials, the Christian had only to denounce his faith and say "Caesar is lord." Some might argue that it would have been better to give recognition to a Roman emperor rather than suffer greatly or watch family members be put to death. However, the demands of Christianity (now, as well as then) are such that a believer can never worship a substitute for the living Christ. When confronted with persecution, any compromise of faith is shameful in the face of those who have testified for Christ with their life. The early Christians understood that there was never a time when they could deny Jesus as their Lord and be justified in doing so. Just as three Hebrew children in the book of Daniel stood before a mighty king and were willing to face suffering rather than deny the only true God

---

[4] Herbert B. Workman, *Persecution in the Early Church* (Cincinnati: Jennings & Graham, 1906), 299-300.

(Dan. 3), so thousands of early Christians where willing to face Roman persecution even if it resulted in their death.

Because persecution was part of the normal Christian experience in the early church, Paul knew there would be Christians who would be tempted to retaliate against their attackers and do evil to those who did evil to them. Unjustified attacks will stimulate the sin nature within the Christian. Because the sin nature is usually the first responder in evil situations, the Christian must be careful to exercise self-restraint and not act impulsively, but control his emotions. The Christian must be governed by God's Word and never by his hot temper, as the Scripture tells him to "be angry, and *yet* do not sin" (Eph. 4:26).

> Never pay back evil for evil to anyone. Respect what is right in the sight of all men. If possible, so far as it depends on you, be at peace with all men. Never take your own revenge, beloved, but leave room for the wrath *of God*, for it is written, "VENGEANCE IS MINE, I WILL REPAY," says the Lord. (Rom. 12:17-19)

It's easy to retaliate and kick the one who kicked you, or hit the one who hit you, or curse the one who cursed you. But this is not the Christian way. Jesus suffered unjustly many times throughout His life, and especially during His illegal trials which led to His crucifixion. And even though He was verbally reviled, "He did not revile in return; while suffering, He uttered no threats, but kept entrusting *Himself* to Him who judges righteously" (1 Pet. 2:23).

> As children of God, we must live on the highest level—returning good for evil. Anyone can return good for good and evil for evil. The only way to overcome evil is with good. If we return evil for evil, we only add fuel to the fire. And even if our enemy is not converted, we have still experienced the love of God in our own hearts and have grown in grace.[5]

The persecuted Christians living in Rome could face their evil attackers with courage because they knew God was in control of their circumstances as well as their eternal destiny. Just as three Hebrew children were able to stand against the pressure of a Babylonian king and face the torment of fire rather than compromise their faith, the Christians living in Rome faced their attackers by trusting

---

[5] Warren Wiersbe, *The Bible Exposition Commentary: New Testament,* Vol. 1, 556.

God and His Word. By faith, the Christian has confidence in the face of suffering because he knows "God causes all things to work together for good to those who love God, to those who are called according to *His* purpose" (Rom. 8:28). Even if the Christian should face death, he knows he will leave this world and come immediately into the presence of the Lord (2 Cor. 5:8), have a new home in heaven (John 14:1-6), receive his resurrection body (1 Cor. 15:51-57; Phil. 3:21), obtain his eternal inheritance (1 Pet. 1:4-5), and enjoy the reality of the eternal life he received at the moment of he trusted Christ as his Savior (John 3:16; 10:28; 1 John 5:10). Jesus Himself stated "do not fear those who kill the body but are unable to kill the soul; but rather fear Him who is able to destroy both soul and body in hell" (Matt. 10:28).

Living in God's will is not always easy, and it does not guarantee a positive response from those who follow worldly values. The teaching of Scripture is that "all who desire to live godly in Christ Jesus will be persecuted" (2 Tim. 3:12). Sadly, there are many Christians who suffer for sinful reasons and it is good that they suffer, if it teaches them humility and respect for legitimate authority. The Apostle Peter tells Christians to "make sure that none of you suffers as a murderer, or thief, or evildoer, or a troublesome meddler; but if *anyone suffers* as a Christian, he is not to be ashamed, but is to glorify God in this name" (1 Pet. 4:15-16). We cannot stop suffering in this life, but "it is better, if God should will it so, that you suffer for doing what is right rather than for doing what is wrong" (1 Pet. 3:17). We cannot control what other people think or how they behave, but we can control our response to them, and we can make sure that what we do is pleasing to the Lord by being obedient-to-the-Word believers. In this way, we can overcome evil by doing God's will for our lives; and this is good.

The Christian cannot control much of the suffering that comes into his life, but he does not have to be overcome by that suffering, as he can look to God and maintain faith in His Word. Jesus was not overcome by the cruelty and suffering he endured, but showed love and forgiveness to His attackers (Luke 23:34), and "who for the joy set before Him endured the cross, despising the shame, and has sat down at the right hand of the throne of God" (Heb. 12:2). Stephen, who spoke strong words of truth while filled with the Holy Spirit, prayed and asked God to forgive those who stoned him to death (Acts 7:60). Paul and Silas demonstrated loving concern for the jailer who kept them in chains, sharing the gospel with him when given the opportunity (Acts 16:22-31). Our lives may be vulnerable to the unjust pain and suffering caused by others, but we must look beyond the suffering and be willing to love even our attackers for the sake of Christ in the hope that they may come to know the gospel and be saved.

As Christians, we must learn to live above our circumstances and find joy in God and His Word rather than the circumstances of this life. Christian joy never fades because God and His Word are eternal and the world cannot touch the soul that clings to them. There is a joy that comes from this world, but it is connected to the temporal things of life and can be lost in a moment or taken away. For many, their joy is dependent on circumstances, and such a joy is always weak because circumstances are unstable and always changing.

> Consider it all joy, my brethren, when you encounter various trials, knowing that the testing of your faith produces endurance. And let endurance have *its* perfect result, so that you may be perfect and complete, lacking in nothing. (Jam. 1:2-4)

Rejoicing in the midst of Christian suffering is an act of the will, not a natural emotional response. By faith the Christian chooses to praise God in the midst of his suffering because he knows God is using that suffering to

46

produce the character of Christ in him (John 16:33; Rom. 5:3-5; Jam. 1:2-4). Even when the Christian faces death at the hands of violent attackers, he is to continually entrust himself to God as the keeper of his soul (Luke 23:46; Acts 7:59).

The Christian overcomes evil when he adopts God's will for his life and follows it, no matter the cost. The Christian overcomes evil by committing himself to doing God's will according to Scripture and refusing to bow down to the evil pressures of weak people who have surrendered themselves to Satan's worldly system. To be sure, overcoming evil is not a onetime event, but a lifetime activity that has application not only in prison, but every aspect of life wherever evil is encountered. The remaining chapters of this book explain four basic activities the Christian needs to learn and incorporate into his life on a regular basis in order to advance spiritually and live strong in the will of God.

1. Submitting to God (Rom. 12:1-2).
2. Learning Scripture (2 Tim. 2:15; 3:16-17).
3. Living by Faith (Rom. 1:17; 10:17).
4. Developing the Spiritual Life (Eph. 5:18; Gal. 5:16).

Overcoming Evil in Prison

Chapter 3

Submission to God

> Submit [Grk. *hupotasso*] therefore to God. Resist
> the devil and he will flee from you. (Jam. 4:7)

The Christian living in prison overcomes evil when
he learns to submit to God and obey His commands. The
Greek verb *hupotasso*—as it is commonly used in
Scripture—means to submit oneself to the legitimate
authority of another. God's authority is supreme since He
is the sovereign Ruler of all creation and there is no one
beyond Him. Christians are commanded to submit to God
as well as some people to whom God has delegated
authority. Biblical examples of submission include Jesus
submitting to God the Father (1 Cor. 15:27-28), Jesus
submitting to His human parents (Luke 2:51), angels
submitting to God (1 Pet. 3:22), the creation submitting to
God (Rom. 8:20; Heb. 2:5, 8), the church submitting to
Jesus Christ (Eph. 1:22), believers submitting to their
pastor (1 Pet. 5:5; Heb. 13:17), the wife submitting to her
husband (Eph. 5:22, 24; Col. 3:18; Tit. 2:5; 1 Pet. 3:1, 5-6),

slaves submitting to their masters (Tit. 2:9; 1 Pet. 2:18), Christians submitting to God (Heb. 12:9; Jas. 4:7), and lastly, Christians submitting to human governmental authorities (Rom. 13:1; Tit. 3:1; 1 Pet. 2:13-14). These last two categories will be the main points of discussion throughout this chapter.

Submission means that one person is surrendering his will to accomplish the will of another. Submitting to God means the Christian is willing to think, say, and do whatever God directs. Scripture reveals that God speaks to all aspects of life including marriage, personal relationships, finances, politics, the military, social issues, science, and other facets of human existence. The believer who is in complete submission to God recognizes His authority over him. Too many Christians compartmentalize God in their lives and want to give Him control over some areas while restricting Him in others. Compartmentalization is sinful because the believer is telling God that He cannot have control over some area of his life. Sin always gets a foothold in the believer to the degree that he refuses to surrender himself to God.

James wrote to Christians who were not living in complete submission to God and he told them "submit therefore to God. Resist the devil and he will flee from you" (Jam. 4:7). At first glance, it might appear that James was telling them to do two separate things: 1) submit to God and, 2) resist the devil. Actually, the first command takes care of the second. By submitting to God the believer is resisting the devil, since he cannot submit both to God and the devil at the same time, nor can he resist both at the same time. Satan very much wants control of a person's life, and to the degree a person says "no" to God, he is saying "yes" to the enemy. There is no middle ground upon which a person can stand, as though there is a neutral place where a person can have control of his life and be neither under God's authority nor under Satan's authority. Each Christian must choose for himself who he will follow at any given moment; and though no one can force him to choose who he will follow, there are consequences for the choices he makes. God always calls the Christian to be obedient both to know and live His Word and resist the temptations of the enemy. Satan pressures the Christian to conform to his worldly system—which, at its core, excludes God and elevates man—and the weak believer yields to Satan's temptations in order to alleviate the pressures that are weighing on him. The Apostle Peter knew what it meant to cave into worldly pressures. After he publicly denied the Lord three times, he "went out and wept bitterly" (Matt. 26:75). There is no joy in the heart of the Christian who turns away from the Lord and yields himself to Satan's pressures.

The Bible tells us "the LORD is righteous, He loves righteousness; the upright will behold His face" (Ps. 11:7). Because God is righteous in character He expects righteous conduct from His children. Submitting to God leads to righteous living; and the devil flees from such a Christian because he knows he cannot gain a foothold in his life. The devil spends his days in search of weaker Christians that he might keep them enslaved to his evil system. The strong believer is the one who is learning and living God's will on a daily basis and striving for righteousness. Such a believer will be effective for the Lord and make an impact wherever he lives.

The Bible clearly commands the Christian to submit to God and to governmental authorities. God has delegated authority to the human governments of this world. To disobey governmental authorities is a sin that carries the threat not only of human punishment but also divine punishment. According to Scripture, human governments are God's agents "sent by him for the punishment of evil doers and the praise of those who do right" (1 Pet. 2:14). Human governments are to do two things: 1) punish those who do evil and, 2) praise those who do right.

> Every person is to be in subjection [*hupotasso*] to the governing authorities. For there is no authority except from God, and those that exist are established by God...Therefore it is necessary to be in subjection [*hupotasso*], not only because of wrath, but also for conscience' sake. (Rom. 13:1, 5)

> Remind them to be subject [*hupotasso*] to rulers, to authorities, to be obedient, to be ready for every good deed. (Tit. 3:1)

> Submit [*hupotasso*] yourselves for the Lord's sake to every institution, whether to a king as the one in authority, or to governors as sent by him for the punishment of evil doers and the praise of those who do right. (1 Pet. 2:13-14)

The believer is commanded to be in submission to governmental authority, and this includes the officers in prison who have their authority from the government. It is interesting that Paul and Peter both wrote the above Scriptures to Christians who were suffering unjustly under the Roman government which was corrupt in many ways;

yet, that government was still ordained by God to serve His purpose in keeping basic justice and order within society. We could read Romans 13:1 as "every person is to be in subjection to the [Roman] governing authorities." Christians are to submit to legitimate governing authorities and show respect at all times (i.e. governmental rulers, police officers, military officers, parents, teachers, coaches, employers, etc.). However, when a human institution oversteps divinely delegated authority and commands the Christian to disobey God, then the Christian has the biblical right and the duty to say "no" to that human authority.

There are biblical examples of believers who have engaged in legitimate civil disobedience to human governments. In every case, when the believer said "no" to governmental authorities, it was because the believer was commanded to do something that directly contradicted God's will. The believer had the greater responsibility of saying "yes" to God, which meant saying "no" to the government. Examples of legitimate civil disobedience include:

1. The mid-wives who disobeyed pharaoh's command to kill all the newborn male Hebrew children (Exodus 1-2).

2. Hananiah, Mishael, and Azariah who disobeyed Nebuchadnezzar's command to worship a golden statue (Daniel 3).
3. Daniel who disobeyed the command to pray to the human king as god (Daniel 6).
4. Peter who disobeyed the command to stop preaching in the name of Jesus (Acts 5:27-29)

In each of the above acts of civil disobedience, believers were commanded by governmental authorities to do something that contradicted God's Word. Human laws that command disobedience to God (i.e. denying Christ) must be distinguished from laws that permit disobedience (i.e. abortion). **The rule for the believer is that he is to obey human authorities so long as those human authorities do not command something that contradicts God's Word.** When there is a conflict between human and divine law, the Christian must obey divine law.

Human authorities should be viewed as protectors and regulators of freedom. When any system of human authority breaks down, it fails to regulate the balance between freedom and law. Law and freedom are necessary for each other. Law without freedom is tyranny. Freedom without law is anarchy. Both law and freedom are complimentary and beneficial, but each without the other is destructive.

The government of the United States of America has its authority from God (Rom. 13:1, 5). The House and Senate propose and vote to pass federal laws with the approval of the President. Individual states pass their own laws, and state police officers enforce many of those laws, arresting violators who will eventually come to a courthouse and stand before a judge. The court determines guilt or innocence and the judge passes judgment where the punishment is ideally equal to the crime. Minor crimes bring a minor punishment; however, if the crime is serious, the person who fractured the law can be sentenced to probation or prison for a determined period of time, after which he is released and then has the opportunity to conform to society and adhere to its basic laws and enjoy the blessing of freedom. If a person fails to adhere to the divinely delegated laws of the land, then by his own decision he forfeits his freedom and will eventually find himself back in jail or prison.

Most inmates in prison understand and have enforced this very legal system within their own home. As a parent, they would convene with the other parent to create laws which, if accepted, would regulate the order of the household. As a parent, they would create and pass laws like the government, and like a police officer would enforce those laws with their children, and as a judge would sometimes execute punishment upon their children, and as a jailer would sometimes make sure the children stay locked in their room until they were ready for release. The parent might even put them on probation and regulate their behavior until such a time as the parent thinks the child is mature and responsible enough to have their full freedom again. Many inmates wrongly despise legitimate authority, yet the irony is that they operate by many of the same rules as the government that put them in prison.

God Himself is the supreme lawgiver. He is repeatedly acknowledged in Scripture as a righteous Ruler and Judge (Ps. 11:7; 19:9; 119:137). However, we must not think of God as a hateful tyrant who creates and enforces laws as a means of suppressing mankind. God has provided His laws to His children for their protection as well as their physical and spiritual wellbeing. God's laws reflect His love and care for others. Just as a loving parent provides laws for their children in order to protect them and teach them what is good and right, so God gives commands to those whom He loves in order that they may be blessed. When a believer understands that God's laws spring from His loving heart, they say with the Psalmist "the law of Your mouth is better to me than thousands of gold and silver *pieces*" (Ps. 119:72), "O how I love Your law! It is my meditation all the day" (Ps. 119:97), and "How sweet are Your words to my taste! *Yes, sweeter* than honey to my mouth!" (Ps. 119:103). God is righteous, and all His commands are righteous, holy, and good.

> The law of the LORD is perfect, restoring the soul; The testimony of the LORD is sure, making wise the simple. The precepts of the LORD are right, rejoicing the heart; The commandment of the LORD is pure, enlightening the eyes. (Ps. 19:7-8)

Even when God disciplines His children because they have been disobedient, He does so out of love. God always punishes His children in love, and always for the purpose of instilling humility and respect. Sometimes the love of God can comfort the suffering believer, and sometimes it is the love of God that brings the suffering! The Scripture declares "my son, do not regard lightly the discipline of the Lord, nor faint when you are reproved by Him; for those whom the Lord loves He disciplines, and He scourges every son whom He receives" (Heb. 12:5-6). Every child of God challenges His authority at some time, and God provides loving discipline to correct him and steer him into the path of righteousness.

> It is for discipline that you endure; God deals with you as with sons; for what son is there whom *his* father does not discipline? But if you are without discipline, of which all have become partakers, then you are illegitimate children and not sons. Furthermore, we had earthly fathers to discipline us, and we respected them; shall we not much rather be subject to the Father of spirits, and live? For they disciplined us for a short time as seemed best to them, but He *disciplines us* for *our* good, so that we may share His holiness. All discipline for the moment seems not to be joyful, but sorrowful; yet to those who have been trained by it, afterwards it yields the peaceful fruit of righteousness. (Heb. 12:7-11)

Whenever God deals with His children, He always deals in love. God is always aware of what His children are doing and He is always in complete control of the outcome. Since God is sovereign, omniscient, omnipotent, and omnipresent, there are no accidents in the life of a Christian. The Christian finds himself in prison basically for one of three reasons:

1. He violated the laws of man which are ordained by God and he is suffering for his crime and needs to learn respect for divinely appointed authority (Rom. 13:1, 5; Tit. 3:1; 1 Pet. 2:13-14; 4:15).
2. He is innocent before man of any wrongdoing, but is guilty before God of violating His Word and is under divine discipline (Heb. 12:4-11). In this case, jail or prison is God's instrument for disciplining the rebellious Christian.
3. He is innocent before both man and God (like Joseph, Job, Peter, Paul and Silas), and God is testing his faith (Gen. 39-41; Job 1:1-2:10; 5:17; Acts 5:40-42; 16:22-25; 1 Pet. 3:17; 4:12-14, 19; Jam. 1:2-4).

In the first two categories the Christian is rightly suffering because of his sin (Heb. 12:4-11; 1 Pet. 4:15); whereas, in the third category, he is suffering for living righteously (Gen. 39-41; Acts 5:40-42; 16:22-25; 1 Pet. 3:17; 4:12-14, 19). Even in category one or two, the Christian can find some joy in knowing that God is disciplining him because He loves him enough to give him what he needs. Once the Christian recognizes God's loving hand of discipline upon him, he can experience joy if he will submit to Him and stop rebelling against the authority of His Word. The Christian who is in category three usually displays an attitude of praise to God because he realizes God is in control of his situation and that he is suffering for righteousness sake (see Job 1:21; 2:10; 13:15; Acts 5:40-41; 16:22-25).

A good example of believers who suffered for righteousness and praised God afterward were Peter and the apostles, who were wrongly commanded by the Jewish authorities "not to continue teaching" in the name of Jesus, to which Peter replied, "we must obey God rather than men" (Acts 5:28, 29). Here was a case of legitimate civil disobedience. After the Jewish authorities received some counsel from a Pharisee named Gamaliel, they agreed to whip the apostles and send them on their way hoping the punishment was severe enough to deter them from further preaching.

> They took his [Gamaliel's] advice; and after calling the apostles in, they flogged them and ordered them not to speak in the name of Jesus, and *then* released them. So they [Peter and the apostles] went on their way from the presence of the Council, rejoicing that they had been considered worthy to suffer shame for *His* name. (Acts 5:40-41)

Overcoming Evil in Prison

Imagine that! Here the apostles get flogged with a whip and then walk away "rejoicing that they had been considered worthy to suffer shame for *His* name" (Acts 5:41). Now, every Christian who is in jail or prison can ask himself what his attitude was when he got there. Was he complaining because he got caught for his crime? Was he whining because he felt like he was getting a raw deal? Or was he praising God because he knew he was suffering for righteousness sake like the apostles? In twelve years of jail ministry I've never met anyone in category three.

Another example of believers who suffered for righteousness sake and praised God afterward were the apostle Paul and his companion Silas, who had been preaching the gospel in the city of Philippi. As a result of some false charges brought against them, a conflict arose with some men of the city and Paul and Silas were treated very severely.

> The crowd rose up together against them, and the chief magistrates tore their robes off them and proceeded to order *them* to be beaten with rods. When they had struck them with many blows, they threw them into prison, commanding the jailer to guard them securely; and he, having received such a

command, threw them into the inner prison and fastened their feet in the stocks. (Acts 16:22-24)

Paul and Silas were doing the will of God by sharing the gospel of Christ, and what did they get for their Christian service? They were attacked, publicly humiliated as their robes were torn off them, and then were beaten with rods and thrown into prison. Yet, after all this horrible unjust treatment, the Scripture tells us "about midnight Paul and Silas were praying and singing hymns of praise to God" (Acts 16:25a). It was their attitude of praise in the midst of their suffering for righteousness that led to the salvation of one of the prison guards. This was all by divine design, as God led Paul and Silas to prison in order to share the gospel with a prison guard who believed in Christ and is now in heaven.

All three categories of suffering previously listed consider the believer only. The Bible speaks to the unbeliever only in regard to God's gift of salvation (Acts 16:30-31). If an unbeliever finds himself in jail, it is often for the purpose of humbling him under the hand of God so that he might be saved by trusting in Christ (John 3:16).

Overcoming Evil in Prison

Divine Discipline Leading to Death

> If anyone sees his [Christian] brother committing a
> sin not *leading* to death, he shall ask and *God* will
> for him give life to those who commit sin not
> *leading* to death. There is a sin *leading* to death. (1
> John 5:16-17)

It happens from time to time that a Christian will
see another Christian "committing a sin." The apostle
John distinguished two kinds of sin in the life of the
Christian: the "sin not *leading* to death" and the "sin
leading to death" (1 John 5:16-17). The "sin not *leading* to
death" is any sin the Christian commits that does not
warrant death from the hand of God, though it may bring
divine discipline if the believer continues in it. When Peter
publicly denied the Lord Jesus three times, it was a terrible
sin, but it was not one that resulted in his death afterwards
(Matt. 26:69-75). When King David had an affair with
Bathsheba and murdered her husband Uriah, it was a
terrible sin, but not one that resulted in his death afterwards
(2 Sam. 12:9-13). The Lord punished David severely for
his sin and told him "I will raise up evil against you from
your own household" (2 Sam. 12:11); however, David was
also informed by Nathan the prophet "you shall not die" (2

64

Sam. 12:13). Peter and David both committed horrible sins, yet they were sins "not *leading* to death."

The Christian can commit a sin, or engage in a sinful lifestyle that results in the Lord taking his life. The sin that leads to death "denotes a sin habitually practiced by a believer, leading to God's removing him from this life, but not taking away his salvation."[1] It refers to the Christian who has become so sinfully rebellious that God disciplines him to point of death and takes him home to heaven. There are references in the Bible where God personally issued the death penalty for one or more of His erring Children who had defied His authority and these examples can be found both in the Old and New Testaments (e.g. Lev. 10:1-3; 2 Sam. 6:1-7; Acts 5:1-11; 1 Cor. 5:1-5; 11:30).

The apostle Paul mentioned three stages of divine discipline when he wrote to Christians at Corinth who were partaking of the Lord's Supper "in an unworthy manner" (1 Cor. 11:27). The Lord's Supper symbolizes the love, humility, and sacrifice the Lord Jesus manifested when He came to earth and took upon Himself perfect humanity (the

---

[1] Paul S. Karleen, *The Handbook to Bible Study: With a Guide to the Scofield Study System* (New York: Oxford University Press, 1987), 359.

unleavened bread) and went to the cross and shed His blood (red juice) for the forgiveness of sins (Mark. 10:45; John 13:1-17; Eph. 1:7; Phil. 2:3-8). However, during the church fellowship, some Christians were sinning by getting drunk and others were selfishly eating all the food and leaving none for the poorer believers (1 Cor. 11:21-22). After such selfish and sinful behavior, these arrogant Christians would then partake of the Lord's Supper! God Himself punished these believers for their arrogance within the church. First, God used warning discipline (weakness), then moved to intensive discipline (sickness), and finally resorted to ultimate discipline (sleep). The term *sleep* is used in the New Testament to refer to believers who have died (John 11:11-14; 1 Cor. 15:51-52). God decided to take the lives of some of these believers due to their failure to correct by self-evaluation their own behavior as inconsistent with the values of the Lord's Supper.

> He [Paul] is specifically teaching that some members of the church at Corinth were weak and others were ill because they would not judge themselves as they should and cleanse themselves, but came unworthily to the Lord's Table, and the result was that God had chastised them. ...There is, indeed, a mysterious phrase 'and many sleep' (1

Cor. 11:30), which means that many were dead because they would not judge themselves.[2]

At the church at Corinth, some believers were judged and put to death by the Lord because of their sin. Other examples of divine judgment leading to death include: doing evil (Gen. 38:7), failure to respect His holiness (Lev. 10:1-3), lying to the Holy Spirit (Acts 5:1-11), and sexual immorality (1 Cor. 5:1-5). For the believer who is in perpetual sin and who does not listen to God, jail or prison can serve to meet the requirements of all three phases of discipline. God is very patient, but His authority will not be rejected by the arrogant believer forever, for He "is able to humble those who walk in pride" (Dan. 4:37).

"Shall not the Judge of all the earth deal justly" when He is dealing with His children (Gen. 18:25)? Yes, God always deals justly with His children! Many Christians are rightfully in prison because they failed to submit to God's authority as well as those human governmental authorities He has established for the good of mankind. As a parent disciplines a child for disobedience, so God disciplines His children for

---

[2] David Martyn Lloyd-Jones, *The Church and the Last Things* (Wheaton, Ill.: Crossway Books, 1998), 56.

disobeying Him (Heb. 12:5-11). Sometimes that discipline comes in the form of jail or prison. God disciplines His children to produce humility that leads to obedience. God commands His children to obey the laws of the land, and failure to submit to human forms of government is failure to submit to God (Rom. 13:1, 5; Tit. 3:1; 1 Pet. 2:13-14)! For the Christian to overcome evil, he absolutely must learn submission to divine and human authority. *Submission* is a good word and needs to be evidenced more in the lives of Christians everywhere.

Chapter 4

Learning Scripture

> Like newborn babies, long for the pure milk of the word, so that by it you may grow in respect to salvation. (1 Pet. 2:2)

A Christian in prison has great potential for spiritual success because he has both time and opportunity to grow in God's Word. Most Christians living in society will tell you they are very busy living from day to day and often find it difficult to devote the time necessary to study God's Word as they ought. The Christian in prison has time, and lots of it. He can make the most of his time by getting into Scripture and learning and applying it daily. This will help his spiritual life during his time in prison as well as his time afterward.

Learning the Word of God necessarily precedes doing the will of God. The Bible provides all the information the believer needs to grow spiritually (1 Cor. 2:10-16; Eph. 1:3-5), walk by faith (Rom. 10:17), and attain Christian maturity (Eph. 4:13; 2 Tim. 3:16-17). As the Christian advances spiritually, he will eventually begin to manifest the fruit of the Holy Spirit (Gal. 5:22-23). I've seen Christians reach spiritual maturity while living in prison, and they would manifest the fruit of the Holy Spirit more often than the fruit of the flesh. No Christian ever reaches a place where he is completely without sin in his life (Eccl. 7:20; 1 Jo. 1:8, 10). However, the spiritual Christian will admit his sin, confess it to God on a regular basis (1 Jo. 1:9), and keep seeking after God through His Word. For the Christian, occasional relapse into sin does not equal collapse of the spiritual life.

Good decisions are rooted in Scripture. As the Christian studies the Bible, he realizes it speaks to every area of life and not just parts of it. God is very thorough and has spoken perfect truth to mankind and provided a wealth of knowledge that will benefit him in everything. The man who closes himself off to God and His Word is spiritually poor; because he is shutting out the wonderful truths that reveal the many spiritual blessings He has provided (Eph. 1:3; cf. Ps. 119:162).

I recommend reading the Bible from Genesis onward, straight through to the book of Revelation, and then start over again. Certainly there are individual books to study, and doctrinal lessons to be gleaned, but it is only from a reading of the whole Bible that the Christian will gain a full sense of who God is, what He has accomplished in history, and where He is taking humanity into the future. Too often men study only parts of the Bible, or get their knowledge about God from Christian books other than Scripture, and this can lead to a limited and/or incomplete understanding of God. I've met Christians who correctly understand that God is love, yet incorrectly think that's all He is, and then have great difficulty understanding concepts such as the Lake of Fire. They struggle within themselves and say "how can a loving God send people to the Lake of Fire?" Yet, if they understood some of God's other attributes such His holiness, righteousness and justice, they would understand the necessity of the Lake of Fire. If one starts in the book of Genesis and reads all the way through the Bible, he will gain a fuller understanding of God and realize that He has many attributes. According to Scripture God is:

1. *Sovereign* – He rules His universe as He pleases (1 Chron. 29:11; Dan. 4:35; Acts 17:24-25).
2. *Righteous* – He is upright in character (Ps. 11:7; 119:137).
3. *Just* – He is upright in all His actions (Ps. 9:7-8; 19:9; 50:6; 58:11).

4. *Holy* – He is positively good and completely set apart from sin (Ps. 99:9).
5. *Omniscient* – He knows all things (Ps. 139:1-6; Matt. 6:31-33).
6. *Omnipresent* – He is everywhere (Ps. 139:7-12; Heb. 13:5).
7. *Omnipotent* – He is all powerful (Job 42:2; Isa. 40:28-29).
8. *Immutable* – He never changes (Ps. 102:26, 27; Mal. 3:6).
9. *Truth* – He is truth and reveals truth (2 Sam. 7:28; John 14:6; 17:17; 1 John 5:20).
10. *Loving* – He acts in the best interest of others (Jer. 31:3; 1 John 4:7-12, 16).
11. *Faithful* – He is consistent to fulfill His promises (Deut. 7:9; Lam. 3:23; 1 John 1:9).
12. *Merciful* – He is compassionate to the needy (Ps. 86:15; Luke 6:36; Tit. 3:5).
13. *Gracious* – He is kind to the undeserving and humble (Ps. 111:4; 116:5; 1 Pet. 5:5, 10).
14. *Eternal* – He forever exists before, beyond, and after time (Deut. 33:27; 1 Tim. 1:17).

The Scripture reveals that God exists as a Trinity: God the Father (Matt. 6:9), God the Son (John 1:1, 14 Matt. 16:16), and God the Holy Spirit (Acts 5:3-4). The

Persons of the Trinity are co-eternal, co-infinite, and co-equal, and though they have differing roles in how they relate to each other and the creation, they are equal in essence. Being equal in essence means that all three Persons of the Godhead share the same attributes mentioned above.

Scripture also reveals that there was a time, nearly two thousand years ago, when God the Son took upon Himself true humanity (Gen. 3:15; John 1:1, 14), was born of a virgin (Isa. 7:14; Matt. 1:18-25), in the chosen line of Abraham and David (Matt. 1:1), born King of the Jews (Matt. 2:2), lived righteously according to the Mosaic Law (Matt. 5:17-19; Gal. 4:4), never sinned (Heb. 4:15), willingly died on a cross in the place of sinners (Mark 10:45; Rom. 5:8), was buried in a grave and rose to life on the third day (1 Cor. 15:3-4), ascended to heaven where He is currently interceding for the saints (Acts 1:10-11; Rom. 8:34), and will return to earth in the future to reign in perfect righteousness (Rev. 19:11-16; 20:1-6). This same Jesus is now providing salvation as a free gift to all who come to Him by grace alone through faith alone (John 3:16; 1 Cor. 15:3-4; Gal. 2:16; Eph. 2:8-9; Phil. 3:9; Tit. 3:5). Without Scripture, we would know nothing of the Person and work of Jesus Christ, and we would not know how to be saved by trusting Him as our Savior.

The Bible reveals how the universe came into existence (Gen. 1-2), that man is special from the rest of the creation because he is made in the image of God (Gen. 1:26-27), the existence of both fallen and unfallen angels (1 Tim. 4:1; Heb. 1:14), what the angel Lucifer was thinking at the time he sinned and led his rebellion against God (Isa. 14:12-14; Ezek. 28:12-18), where sin comes from and why the universe is cursed (Gen. 3:1-24; Rom 8:22), why all men are born sinners (Rom. 5:12; 1 Cor. 15:21-22), how God alone solved the sin problem through the substitutionary death of His Son (Isa. 53; John 3:16-18; Rom. 3:23-26; 5:6-8; 1 Cor. 15:3-4; 2 Cor. 5:17-21; Gal. 2:16; Eph. 2:8-9; Phil. 3:9; Col. 2:13-14; Tit. 3:5; Heb. 2:9; 1 John 2:2; 4:10), and that God will eventually destroy the universe and create a new heavens and new earth where only righteousness exists (Rev. 21-22). These are but a few of the wonderful truths revealed in God's Word that help form a biblical worldview and lead the Christian to see life from the divine perspective. Scripture pulls back the curtain and gives us glimpses into realities we could never come to know on our own except that God has spoken and given us absolute truth.

Study for Yourself

> Be diligent to present yourself approved to God as a workman who does not need to be ashamed, accurately handling the word of truth. (2 Tim. 2:15)

The Christian must study the Bible for himself and try to understand what each human author intended when he wrote to his original audience. The science of interpretation is commonly called hermeneutics, from the Greek word *hermeneuo*, which means to *explain* or *interpret*. Hermeneutics is the working out of rules and methodologies for interpreting biblical texts. The best way to interpret the Bible is to read it normally, like any other book, and to give attention to the original languages, history and culture from which the human author wrote. This method of hermeneutics is commonly called the historical-grammatical approach to learning the Bible because it seeks to understand the Bible from the time and culture from which it was originally written.

Because we are separated from the people and events of Scripture by several thousand years, and because there is so much information, it becomes a difficult task to learn all there is to know in the Bible. We start by reading it for ourselves and getting what we can from the text, and then look to Bible teachers who have devoted themselves to a lifetime of study and become experts in the original languages, history and culture of the Bible. Many excellent Bible scholars have written helpful books which serve as tools to the serious student of the Bible.[1] Here are a few basic points everyone Christian should know about the Bible and hermeneutics:

1. The Bible is a collection of sixty-six books, written by approximately forty human authors over a period of 1500 years.
2. The Bible is special revelation about God and His will for all mankind.
3. The Bible is inspired in the sense that there are no errors or faults in the original Hebrew and Greek texts.
4. There is theological continuity to Scripture because God the Holy Spirit was behind each human author, superintending their writings, making certain that what was written was exactly what He intended; and He did this without removing their personal literary style or choice of vocabulary.

---

[1] A list of reliable and helpful resources is provided in Appendix A.

5. Never make a passage say something that it does not say within its context (e.g. Josh. 24:15; 2 Chron. 7:14; Jer. 29:11; Matt 24: 13-14; John 21: Rev. 3:20).

6. Spiritually gifted pastors and teachers are necessary in the church to help Christians understand the Bible (Eph. 4:11-17). Christian teachers are not infallible, so their teaching must be verified (Acts 17:10-11; 2 Tim. 2:15). A teacher should try to teach in such a way that the student can research the information for himself and verify what is taught.

The Christian should come to the Bible expecting to learn something from God, but it is helpful if he asks the right questions. Below is a list of basic questions every Christian can ask when he studies Scripture:

1. Who is the human author (Moses, David, Paul, Peter)?
2. Who is the audience (a person or group)?
   a. Are they believers?
   b. Are they unbelievers?
   c. Are they a mixed group of saved and lost?
3. What is the subject about which the author is writing (law, war, sin, the gospel)?

4. Are there historical or cultural issues to be aware of (how were women or slaves treated)?
5. Are there important words that need to be inspected closer (i.e. verbs, nouns, prepositions, theological words, etc.)?
6. Are there other passages in the Bible that speak about the subject (i.e. marriage, parenting, war, faith, etc.)?
7. Is there a timeless truth to be drawn from the passage (i.e. God is always faithful, God always speaks truth, sin is never right, man is lost without God, etc.)?
8. Can I apply this biblical truth to my life? We should realize that at times God spoke to certain people at certain times and the truth He spoke to them can never be applied to us today (e.g. the command God gave to Adam and Eve in the Garden of Eden not to eat the fruit of the tree of the knowledge of good and evil; or the command to Israel to sacrifice animals, etc.).
9. How do I apply this truth to my life? This is a very important question, but should always be the last question, after we have studied what Scripture meant to the original audience.

Having a good hermeneutical system for studying

the Scriptures is necessary for understanding. Reading the Bible consistently in a plain or normal way helps the Christian understand it the way God intended. For example, there were hundreds of prophecies that were literally fulfilled regarding the birth, life, death, and resurrection of Jesus Christ, and only a plain reading of these passages make sense (e.g. Ps. 16:9-10; 22:1, 15-18; 31:5; 34:20; 68:18; Isa. 9:1-2, 6; 53:1-12; 61:1; Mic. 5:2; Zech. 13:7; Mal. 3:1). Certainly there are figures of speech, poetry, symbols, parables, and other forms of literary expression in Scripture that human authors used when writing under the divine inspiration of the Holy Spirit; however, even these are plainly seen and understood by the reader as he reads the Bible in a normal way.

> When the plain sense of Scripture makes common sense, seek no other sense; therefore, take every word at its primary, ordinary, usual, and literal meaning unless the facts of the immediate context, studied in the light of related passages and axiomatic [obvious] and fundamental truths, clearly indicate otherwise.[2]

It is important to understand that even the best

---

[2] David L. Cooper, *The God of Israel* (Los Angeles: Biblical Research Society, 1945), iii.

hermeneutical rules consistently applied are not enough to bring about a correct and full understanding of the Bible. We have Scripture to read for ourselves, but the Holy Spirit is the One who helps us to understand it fully and be persuaded to walk in its light. We have God's revelation, but only the Holy Spirit gives illumination. Illumination is "that influence or ministry of the Holy Spirit which enables all who are in right relation with God to understand the Scriptures."[3]

> In illumination the Holy Spirit's work is not only to show what the Bible means, but also to persuade Christians of its truth. Illumination is the Spirit's work, enabling Christians to discern the meaning of the message and to welcome and receive it as from God.[4]

The biblical teaching is that only the Christian who has the indwelling Holy Spirit can fully know the things of God as they are revealed in Scripture. The indwelling Holy Spirit provides the Christian the capacity to fully understand and accept spiritual truths that would otherwise

---

[3] Lewis S. Chafer, "Revelation" *Bibliotheca Sacra*, 94 (1937): 268.

[4] Roy B. Zuck, "The Work of the Holy Spirit in Illumination" *Bibliotheca Sacra*, 141 (1984): 125.

be out of reach. Spiritual truths that once were confusing to the unbeliever prior to salvation are made known and acceptable by the Holy Spirit after he is born again. Paul spoke about this when he wrote to Christians at the church at Corinth.

> Now we have received, not the spirit of the world, but the Spirit who is from God, so that we may know the things freely given to us by God, which things we also speak, not in words taught by human wisdom, but in those taught by the Spirit, combining spiritual *thoughts* with spiritual *words*. (1 Cor. 2:13-14)

The unsaved person cannot know the greater truths of God's Word, no matter how hard he tries. Because the unbeliever does not have the Holy Spirit within him, the result is that he "does not accept the things of the Spirit of God, for they are foolishness to him; and he cannot understand them, because they are spiritually appraised" (1 Cor. 2:14). To be clear, it's not that the unbeliever chooses to misunderstand the things of God, as though it's a matter of choice, but that he "cannot understand them" because he lacks the spiritual capacity altogether.

For the believer, there is a connection between learning Scripture and having a desire to serve God. A rebellious heart can obstruct a person's understanding of Scripture (John 7:17; cf. Ps. 119:34). Carnality can also impede a believer's ability to learn Scripture since he is operating by his sin nature rather than the guidance of the Holy Spirit (1 Cor. 3:1-3). The newborn Christian is to be taught basic doctrines of the Bible (i.e. milk); however, advanced doctrines are only open to the maturing believer who is studying and applying God's Word on a regular basis (i.e. meat; see Heb. 5:12-16).

Apply the Scripture to Your Life

Christianity is not a spectator sport! Scripture teaches that we are to be "doers of the word, and not merely hearers who delude themselves" (Jam. 1:22). Learning by itself is not enough, as we must apply God's Word to our situations. We must love (1 Cor. 13:4-8; 1 John 3:23), forgive (Matt. 18:21-22), pray (1 Thess. 5:17), speak truth (Eph. 4:15, 25), and live by grace (Col. 4:6; Tit. 2:11-13). These are but a few of the many Christian activities Scripture commands us to apply every moment of every day. There are many Christians who have made that very important first step in learning God's Word—and it is a very important and necessary step—but it is only the beginning, as knowledge of Scripture must be applied if there is to be any benefit to the Christian and if God is to be glorified. Jesus pointed this out very clearly when He stated:

> Therefore everyone who hears these words of Mine [receives Scripture] and acts on them [applies what he learns], may be compared to a wise man who built his house on the rock, "And the rain fell, and the floods came, and the winds blew and slammed against that house: and yet it did not fall, for it had been founded on the rock. "Everyone who hears these words of Mine [receives Scripture] and does not act on them [fails to apply what he learns], will be like a foolish man who built his house on the sand. "The rain fell, and the floods came, and the winds blew and slammed against that house; and it fell—and great was its fall." (Matt. 7:24-27)

The wise man is the one who both learns and lives Scripture, whereas the foolish man is the one who hears but fails to apply what he's learned. The storms of life come upon everyone, but it is only the believer who learns and lives by God's Word that is able to stand against life's pressures because his house is built on a solid foundation. God has sent forth His Word and it will accomplish what He desires (Isa. 55:11); yet, at the same time, every Christian is commanded to "let the word of Christ richly dwell within you, with all wisdom teaching and admonishing one another with psalms and hymns and spiritual songs, singing with thankfulness in your hearts to God" (Col. 3:16). God's Word is "living and active" (Heb. 4:12), but it must be studied (2 Tim. 2:15), received (Jam. 1:21), and acted upon for there to be personal benefit in the Christian life (Matt. 7:24-27).

As the Christian studies Scripture on a regular basis, paying attention to the plain meaning of the text, he will advance in his understanding of God as well as the many blessings He has provided. The Christian will see God's Word as beneficial for providing an understanding of the gospel message (John 3:16; 1 Cor. 15:3-4), encouraging the believer to walk in truth (Ps. 86:11; 119:97-106), to know God's will (Rom. 12:1-2), to build his faith (Rom. 10:17), to bring spiritual sanctification (Ps. 119:9-11; John 17:17), to provide a stable life (Matt. 7:24-27), to show the weakness of man (Jer. 17:5), to reveal the strength of God (Jer. 17:7), to provide a stable and righteous life (Ps. 1:1-3), to teach divine viewpoint (Isa. 55:7-9), to give wisdom (Prov. 2:6-14), to give confidence (Isa. 41:10), to protect from satanic and demonic influence (Matt. 4:1-11; 2 Cor. 11:3; Eph. 6:10-13), and to lead to spiritual maturity (Eph. 4:11-16; 2 Tim. 3:16-17; Heb. 5:13-14; 1 Pet. 2:2). These are but a sampling of the many benefits of a life that is invested in God's Word.

The growing Christian is one who is learning God's Word in order to live God's will. This is always the order of things. God has given His revelation to man, but it must be studied and applied if there is to be any benefit at all. The gospel is learned and the sinner believes in Christ for salvation. The Christian learns God's Word and is blessed when he lives by faith, obeying His commands and trusting His promises.

Overcoming Evil in Prison

Chapter 5

Living by Faith

The Christian living in prison overcomes evil when he learns to live by faith in God and His Word. Faith is the act of trusting or relying on someone or something, most often for the sake of personal benefit. Faith in God is a response to commands or promises He has given. When Abram was 75 years old God commanded him to "go forth from your country, and from your relatives and from your father's house, to the land which I will show you" (Gen. 12:1), and Abram responded positively to the divine command and "went forth as the LORD had spoken to him" (Gen. 12:4). What the Lord commanded of Abram, by faith he obeyed. Faithful obedience is always the proper response to a divine command. The benefit for Abram obeying the Lord was the divine promise:

> And I will make you a great nation, And I will bless you, And make your name great; And so you shall be a blessing; And I will bless those who bless you, And the one who curses you I will curse. And in

you all the families of the earth will be blessed. (Gen. 12:2-3)

Abram waited years for the son the Lord had promised. One evening God came to Abram in a vision and addressed his concerns about the lack of an heir and said, "now look toward the heavens, and count the stars, if you are able to count them. ...so shall your descendants be" (Gen. 15:5). The scripture then gives Abram's response as, "he believed in the LORD; and He reckoned it to him as righteousness" (Gen. 15:6).

> Abram was already a believer as of Genesis 11-12 when he obeyed God to leave Ur of the Chaldees. This verse is a general statement concerning Abram's life of faith, since his belief in Jehovah was already clear from 12:1 and probably even earlier, at the end of chapter 11. The content of Abram's faith was what he heard and understood directly from God.[1]

On that same evening, God ratified His promises to Abram with a covenant (Heb. *berith* – a contract). Abram

---

[1]Arnold G. Fruchtenbaum, *The Book of Genesis: Exposition from a Messianic Jewish Perspective* (San Antonio, TX. Ariel Ministries, 2009), 275.

finally received the promised son (Isaac) when he was 100 years old, a quarter of a century after receiving by faith the initial promise given to him when he left his homeland under divine orders. Faith clings to the commands and promises of God, often in spite of circumstances or long periods of waiting.

The Christian is one who, like Abram, has trusted God at His Word (John 3:16; 14:6; Acts 16:31; Eph. 2:8-9). God has promised that whoever believes in Christ as Savior "shall not perish, but have eternal life" (John 3:16). Salvation is entirely through faith alone in Christ alone, as the believer is helpless to save himself and comes to the Savior on the basis of unmerited favor (i.e. grace). Once saved, the faith that was exercised in Christ for salvation is the same faith that sustains the believer during his Christian walk. At salvation, the Person of Christ was the object trusted and eternal life was the benefit. Once saved, God's commands and promises in Scripture are the object trusted and the believer's spiritual health is the benefit. God is glorified, both in salvation and the believer's spiritual health.

Biblically, faith is never a blind leap into the unknown, but a thoughtful act of the will by the believer who hears and understands God's Word and responds positively. Scripture tells us, "faith *comes* from hearing, and hearing by the word of Christ" (Rom. 10:17; cf. 14:23; Heb. 4:2; Jas. 1:22). The healthy Christian life always starts by learning God's Word, and once learned, is applied by faith, moment by moment, as long as the Christian lives in this world. The word *faith* is used three ways in Scripture:

1. *Pistis* (Grk. noun) refers to what is believed and often points to a *body of teaching* (Acts 14:22; 16:5; Rom. 14:22; Gal. 1:23).
2. *Pisteuo* (Grk. verb) refers to the *act of believing* and means *to believe, trust,* or *have confidence* in something or someone (John 3:15, 16, 18, 36; 20:31).
3. *Pistos* (Grk. adjective) describes someone as *faithful, reliable,* or *trustworthy* and is used both of man (Matt. 25:23; Col. 1:7; Heb. 3:5), and God (1 Cor. 1:9; 10:13; Heb. 10:23).

Faith, as a verb, demands an object, as it must have something or someone upon which to rest. To receive salvation, the unbeliever is told to "believe in the Lord Jesus, and you will be saved" (Acts 16:31a). To be clear, faith does not save; God saves! Faith is merely the means by which the unsaved person receives salvation, as God alone does the saving. It's just like the faith a person has when he sits down in a chair; his faith does not keep him from crashing to the floor, the chair does. The chair gets all the credit for keeping him from falling. Though a person may exercise faith and receive a benefit, the object always gets the credit, and in the case of our salvation or spiritual health (i.e. our benefit), it is God alone who gets the glory.

Once saved, God does not take the Christian immediately to heaven, but leaves him in a fallen world to advance to spiritual maturity and to serve as His representative to others. While living in the world the Christian will, out of necessity, have to trust in things and people, even though these regularly fail. Scripture teaches that people fail (Jer. 17:5), money fails (Ps. 62:10), and governments fail (Ps. 146:3), and the person who puts complete trust in them is a fool. Yet, people, things, and institutions must be trusted to some degree in order for life to progress and harmony to exist. From Scripture, the Christian realizes that humanity is prone to weakness and failure due to sin; therefore, he relies as little as possible on people and turns to God instead. If he's wise, the Christian will not even look to himself as a source of strength and guidance, knowing himself to be weak and unable to stand against the greater pressures of life. The Christian who lives by faith has admitted his weakness and turned to God for guidance and strength. Humility is necessary for spiritual advance and perpetuating a life of faith.

The apostle Paul was a great man, but he was intentionally made weak by the Lord who gave him a "thorn in the flesh" for the purpose of humbling him (2 Cor. 12:7). Paul does not say what his "thorn in the flesh" was, but it obviously caused him problems and made him weak by human standards. Like any man, the apostle Paul prayed several times for the Lord to take it away, but the Lord told him no.

And He has said to me, "My grace is sufficient for you, for power is perfected in weakness." Most gladly, therefore, I will rather boast about my weaknesses, so that the power of Christ may dwell in me. Therefore I am well content with weaknesses, with insults, with distresses, with persecutions, with difficulties, for Christ's sake; for when I am weak, then I am strong. (2 Cor. 12:9-10)

By faith, the apostle Paul accepted the "thorn in the flesh" the Lord placed on him, because he understood its spiritual value. Paul did not like being made weak, but it was only in his weakness that he sought the Lord for strength. Often the Christian wants God to take away his suffering, yet it's that very suffering that keeps the believer close to the Lord! Why would God take away the very thing that keeps the believer humble and keeps him coming back to God for strength and guidance? The wise and humble believer learns to live by faith and say with the apostle Paul "most gladly, therefore, I will rather boast about my weaknesses, so that the power of Christ may dwell in me" (2 Cor. 12:9). The world does not understand such boasting; but then, the world does not know God.

As the Christian grows in his biblical faith he will submit to God (Rom. 12:1), claim promises (Rom. 8:28; 1 John 1:9), give his concerns to God (1 Pet. 5:6-7), not surrender to fear (Deut. 31:6-8; Isa. 41:10-13), love others (1 Thess. 4:9), rejoice in difficult circumstances (Rom. 5:3-5; 1 Thess. 5:16; Jam. 1:2-4), pray continually (1 Thess. 5:17), be thankful to the Lord (1 Thess. 5:18), and develop a relaxed mental attitude (Isa. 26:3; Phil. 4:11-13). These are but a few of the experiences he will have as he lives by faith. Over time, the Christian's faith will be tested as he faces opportunities to grow in his relationship with the Lord (1 Pet. 1:7), and in everything, he will learn that faith is the only thing that pleases God (Heb. 11:6).

At times, living by faith means the believer does

nothing more than trust God to do what He promised, as when the Lord told the Israelites (who were fleeing for their lives from the Egyptian army), "do not fear! Stand by and see the salvation of the LORD which He will accomplish for you today" (Ex. 14:13). As the Israelites stood by the shore of the Red Sea, they were to do nothing against the Egyptians, but rather watch the Lord do what He'd promised, for He said, "the LORD will fight for you while you keep silent" (Ex. 14:14). In this example, the Israelites lived by faith and rejoiced afterwards as God destroyed their enemies by drowning them in the Red Sea (Ex. 14:16-31; cf. the Song of Moses in Exodus 15).

At the Red Sea, the Israelites performed marvelously by trusting God to do what He'd promised. However, during the forty years of wilderness wanderings the Israelites complained to God over and over rather than live by faith, even though they had His promises in which He said He would provide and care for them. These same believers, who at one time saw God deliver them from their enemies, later doubted Him on a regular basis. The writer of Hebrews picks up on this failure by Old Testament believers and warns his Christian readers to "take care, brethren, that there not be in any one of you an evil, unbelieving heart that falls away from the living God" (Heb. 3:12). God's promises and commands must be accepted and followed by faith; otherwise, there is no benefit to the believer!

> Therefore, let us fear if, while a promise remains of entering His rest, any one of you may seem to have come short of it. For indeed we [Christians] have had good news preached to us, just as they also [Israelites living in the wilderness]; but the word they heard did not profit them, because it was not united by faith in those who heard. (Heb. 4:1-2)

It is a disaster when a believer fails to live by faith, especially since the Lord has made provision for every trial of life (1 Cor. 10:13). Sadly, many believers have failed to claim God's promises and suffered needlessly, and this is what the Scripture is referring to when it says "the word they heard did not profit them, because it was not united by faith in those who heard" (Heb. 4:2). Having God's promises is no guarantee the believer will trust in them. Trusting in God's promises or commands does not always alleviate life's problems, but it does provide the believer the ability to cope with them.

Living by faith sometimes means the believer does nothing but trust in the Lord to do exactly what He said (Ex. 14:13-14); however, there are times when Scripture commands the believer to do something, and this is why James told his readers to "prove yourselves doers of the word, and not merely hearers who delude themselves" (Jam. 1:22). Obeying God's Word is an act of faith. The believer learns what is commanded in Scripture and then decides, by faith, to obey God's will as it has been revealed. Sometimes this calls for personal action and sometimes it calls for no action at all. Discernment is learned over time as the Christian advances spiritually.

Another truth provided in Scripture is that living by faith may result in great blessing, and other times may result in great suffering. The believer is not to concern himself with the end result of either blessing or suffering, but is to live by faith and advance toward spiritual maturity. In Hebrews chapter 11, the writer shares both the blessing and suffering aspects of those who lived by faith. Regarding some of the blessings he says:

> And what more shall I say? For time will fail me if I tell of Gideon, Barak, Samson, Jephthah, of David and Samuel and the prophets, who by faith conquered kingdoms, performed *acts of* righteousness, obtained promises, shut the mouths of lions, quenched the power of fire, escaped the edge of the sword, from weakness were made

96

strong, became mighty in war, [and] put foreign armies to flight. (Heb. 11:32-34)

Every Christian loves to hear the victory stories of those who lived by faith and overcame the adversities of life as God rescued them from their trouble. The Bible is encouraging because there are many victory stories and the Christian needs to hear them. God blesses the believer with many victories that result in deliverance and blessing. However, there are times when the Christian lives by faith in God and is obedient to His Word only to suffer great persecution and die at the hands of violent men. Regarding those who suffered for their faith the writer of Hebrews states:

> ...others were tortured, not accepting their release, so that they might obtain a better resurrection; and others experienced mockings and scourgings, yes, also chains and imprisonment. They were stoned, they were sawn in two, they were tempted, they were put to death with the sword; they went about in sheepskins, in goatskins, being destitute, afflicted, ill-treated (*men* of whom the world was not worthy), wandering in deserts and mountains and caves and holes in the ground. (Heb. 11:35-38)

Overcoming Evil in Prison

Faith in God is no guarantee the believer will live a life free from suffering or persecution. Too many preachers speak of the blessings of the Lord and the victories to be had while dismissing those clear passages in Scripture that speak about Christian suffering which is according to the will of God (1 Pet. 2:19-21; 3:14, 17; 4:19). The growing Christian lives by faith in God, trusting His promises and obeying His commands, whether it requires him to sit still or be active. Sometimes being quiet and doing nothing is just as much an act of faith as speaking out and being busy (Ps. 46:10; Jam. 1:19). The believer learns discernment as he grows in wisdom.

The mind is very much like a garden that must be tended on a regular basis. What is sown is what is reaped. Where there is no faith, weeds will grow and worldly trash will settle. Without faith in God, the Christian is left to look to himself and the things of this world to sustain him, and soon realizes the pressures around him are simply too great to bear. Where Scripture is absent, pleasures are often pursued, but these fail over time, like everything else in life. Eventually, worldly pressures wear a person down, leaving only emptiness inside, or worse, a deep rooted sense of despair. Where God and His Word are absent, in that place darkness will settle. When the believer looks away from the Lord and becomes fixed on the things of this world he will find himself full of anxiety; however, relapse does not have to lead to collapse, as the believer can turn back to God and live by faith. God wants the Christian to have joy (Neh. 8:10), peace (Is. 26:3), love (1 Jo. 4:16-17), contentment (Phil. 4:11-13), and every other attitude related to the abundant life (John 10:10). Only through faith can the Christian know the blessings that belong to him. This takes time, study, and a willingness to trust God at His Word. Without faith, the Christian cannot win; but with faith, he can only win.

Overcoming Evil in Prison

Chapter 6

Developing the Spiritual Life

Every Christian is to live spiritually unto the Lord, offering "spiritual sacrifices acceptable to God through Jesus Christ" (1 Pet. 2:5). The Christian in prison is able to live spiritually just as much as the pastor in the local church or the professor in the seminary classroom. The inmate's geographical location or social status does not hinder his spiritual life at all. God the Father gives the Holy Spirit to every believer at the moment of salvation (1 Cor. 3:16; 6:19), and blesses him "with every spiritual blessing in the heavenly *places* in Christ" (Eph. 1:3). At the moment the Christian is *born again* he is endowed with everything he needs to live spiritually and to fulfill all of his duties as a royal priest living in the Church Age (Rev. 1:6), which duties include:

1. The giving of one's body for service to the Lord (Rom. 12:1-2).
2. The sacrifice of praise for worship (Heb. 13:15).

3. The doing of good works and sharing with others (Heb. 13:16; cf. Phil. 4:18).
4. The sacrifice of one's life for the benefit of others (Phil. 2:17; cf. Phil. 1:21-26).
5. The walk of sacrificial love (Eph. 5:1-2; cf. 1 Pet. 1:22).

The dynamic of the believer's spiritual walk is predicated to a large degree on how much Bible knowledge resides in his soul. He cannot live what he does not know, and learning God's Word necessarily precedes living His will. Knowing God's Word does not guarantee a spiritual walk, as the believer may follow the world rather than the Holy Spirit (Jas. 4:17; 1 Jo. 2:15). Knowing the truth does not mean the believer will walk in it; however, the Christian cannot be spiritual without some knowledge of Scripture, and the more he knows, the more he's able to surrender his life to God and accomplish His will.

The Holy Spirit came to minister in the world in a special way on the day of Pentecost (Acts 2). The ministry of the Holy Spirit is different today than it was for believers who were living under the Mosaic Law. Under the Mosaic Law the Holy Spirit indwelt and empowered only a few believers such as Artisans (Ex. 31:1-5), Judges (Num. 11:25-29; Jud. 3:9-10), Prophets (Ezek. 2:2), and

Kings (1 Sam. 10:6; 16:13). In the current Church Age, every believer is indwelt by the Holy Spirit (John 14:16-17; 1 Cor. 6:19), and that indwelling is permanent because the believer is "sealed in Him with the Holy Spirit of promise, who is given as a pledge of our inheritance, with a view to the redemption of *God's own* possession, to the praise of His glory" (Eph. 1:13-14; cf. 2 Cor. 1:21-22).

> The *fact* of the indwelling Spirit is not revealed through any experience whatsoever; nevertheless that fact is the foundation upon which all other ministries to the child of God must depend. It is impossible for one to enter into the plan of God and provision for a life of power and blessing and ignore the distinct revelation as to *where* the Spirit is now related to the believer. It must be understood and fully believed that the Spirit is now *indwelling* the true child of God and that He indwells from the moment the believer is saved.[1]

Since the Day of Pentecost, the Holy Spirit is working in the lives of all unbelievers to convince them that Jesus Christ is the only Savior (John 16:8-11), and that

---

[1] Lewis S. Chafer, *He that is Spiritual* (Grand Rapids, Mich. Zondervan Publishing, 1967), 33.

by grace alone through faith alone the worst of sinners may come to have eternal life (John 3:16; 10:28). The Holy Spirit is not working to convince the unbeliever of every sin, but only one sin, "because they do not believe in Me" (John 16:9). If a person rejects Christ as Savior and chooses death over life, he then falls under the restraining work of the Holy Spirit who holds back the lawless and destructive behavior of all those reside in spiritual darkness (2 Thess. 2:7).

The Holy Spirit's pre-evangelistic work may be resisted by the unbeliever, but it cannot be stopped. The Christian should never argue with the unbeliever about the gospel of Jesus Christ (2 Tim. 2:24-25), but simply present the facts of Scripture and trust the Holy Spirit to do the rest (1 Cor. 15:3-4). Too many Christians have tried to argue and wrestle the unbeliever into salvation, and this has resulted in frustration for everyone. The Christian is called to be a light, not make people see the light, as the latter is only something God can do (Luke 24:45; Acts 16:14; 2 Cor. 4:3-4).

Once a person believes in Jesus for salvation, he is then delivered "from the domain of darkness, and transferred...to the kingdom of His beloved Son" (Col. 1:13). This transference is instantaneous and permanent.

Once saved, the child of God instantly becomes a "new creature" in Christ Jesus (1 Cor. 5:17), with the spiritual capacity to live righteously (Rom. 6:11-14). The Holy Spirit permanently indwells the Christian and then works from the day of salvation onward to form the character of Christ in him. Some of the instantaneous work that occurs in the life of every Christian at the moment of salvation includes:

1. Regeneration (John 3:6; 2 Cor. 5:17; Col. 2:13).
2. Indwelling each believer (John 14:16-17; Rom. 5:5; 8:9; 1 Cor. 6:19).
3. Baptizing into union with Christ (1 Cor. 12:13; Gal. 3:27).
4. Sealing each believer with the Holy Spirit (Eph. 4:30).
5. Providing eternal life (John 3:16).
6. Imputing Christ's righteousness (2 Cor. 5:21; Phil. 3:9).
7. Providing every spiritual blessing (Eph. 1:3).
8. Providing a spiritual gift for the edification of others (Rom. 12:4-8; 1 Cor. 12:27-31; Eph. 4:11).

The wonderful spiritual riches God bestows on the believer at the moment of salvation are a joy to discover and experience. God has given the Christian everything he needs to live the spiritual life, and no prison wall or evil environment can suppress the Holy Spirit or His work. On many occasions I've witnessed the work of the Holy Spirit in the lives of prison inmates who were sharing the gospel, walking in the Spirit, praying, singing hymns, giving thanks, and living in joy despite their environment. These believers were truly a light in a dark place, and the light of God's Word shone bright in their hearts and lives. They were not sinless believers, but they were humble and honest, willing to confess their sin and get right with God when they had a moment of relapse into the flesh (1 John 1:9; cf. Ps. 32:3-5).

After salvation, the Holy Spirit continually works in the life of the Christian until he leaves this world for heaven. It should be noted that the ongoing work of the Holy Spirit requires obedience from the Christian if there is to be any fruit at all. The Spirit does not force Himself on the Christian, but calls him to a daily walk of fellowship together to accomplish the will of God the Father. After salvation, some of the ongoing work of the Holy Spirit includes:

1. Glorifying Jesus in the believer's life (John 16:14).
2. Teaching through Scripture and gifted spiritual speakers/writers (John 16:13-15; Eph. 4:11-16).

3. Recalling Scripture to the believer's mind (John 14:26; 16:13).
4. Filling the believer (i.e. empowering and guiding; Eph. 5:18).
5. Sustaining the believer's spiritual walk (Gal. 5:16, 25).
6. Illuminating the mind by making Scripture understandable (1 Cor. 2:11-13).
7. Promoting the use of the believer's spiritual gift (Rom. 12:6-8; 1 Cor. 12:4-10, 28-30; Eph. 4:11).

The above list provides the major activities of the Holy Spirit in the life of the Christian after salvation, and they are all positive things the Holy Spirit is doing in the church age. All of these activities require the believer to comply with the Spirit's ongoing ministry. Unfortunately, the Christian can say "no" to the Holy Spirit, and this happens when he grieves and/or quenches the Holy Spirit's activity in his life (Eph. 4:30; 1 Thess. 5:19).

The Christian faces temptations of every imaginable kind because he lives in a fallen world that is currently controlled by Satan, whose societies and institutions are under his evil influence. Temptation is not sin, but the opportunity and enticement to sin. When the Christian commits sin, he does so against the guidance of the Holy

Spirit. Grieving the Holy Spirit occurs when the Christian knowingly commits sin.

> The Scriptures often testify to the fact that the Spirit of God is holy and that He is a person. The indwelling presence of this holy person constitutes the body of a believer a temple of God. In the nature of the case, the presence of sin in any form grieves the Holy Spirit. Accordingly, when the Christian is exhorted to "grieve not the Holy Spirit of God, in whom ye were sealed unto the day of redemption" (Eph. 4:30), it is an appeal to allow nothing in his life contrary to the holiness of the Spirit. It is clear that the one cause of grieving the Holy Spirit is sin.[2]

Quenching the Holy Spirit "may simply be defined as being unyielded to Him, or saying, 'No.' The issue is, therefore, the question of willingness to do His will."[3] The Christian quenches the Holy Spirit in his life when he refuses to follow His directions to pray, worship, love, serve, or engage in any other activity the Scripture teaches. Because the Holy Spirit is never removed from us due to

---

[2] John F. Walvoord, *The Holy Spirit* (Grand Rapids, MI., Zondervan Publishing, 1977), 200.

[3] Ibid., 197.

sin, He is therefore quenched "in the sense of resisting or opposing His will."[4]

Be Filled with the Spirit & Walk by the Spirit

> And do not get drunk with wine, for that is dissipation, but be filled with the Spirit. (Eph. 5:18)

> But I say, walk by the Spirit, and you will not carry out the desire of the flesh. (Gal. 5:16)

The Christian is called to "be filled with the Spirit" and to "walk by the Spirit" (Eph. 5:18; Gal. 5:16). These are two commands that are very important to understand and help to keep the Christian's spiritual life on track and headed in the right direction. The believer who is filled with the Spirit and walking by the Spirit will know what it means to live the victorious life.

Throughout Scripture, the word "filled" (Grk. *pleroo*) means to be guided, controlled or influenced by something or someone (Acts 5:3, 17; 19:28-29). To "be filled with the Spirit" means the believer is being

---

[4] Ibid., 197.

influenced or directed by the Holy Spirit. The Holy Spirit always directs the believer to right thinking and right behavior in accordance with Holy Scripture. Regarding the filling of the Holy Spirit, Warren Wiersbe sates:

> "Be filled with the Spirit" is God's command, and He expects us to obey. The command is plural, so it applies to all Christians and not just to a select few. The verb is in the present tense—"keep on being filled"—so it is an experience we should enjoy constantly and not just on special occasions. And the verb is passive. We do not fill ourselves but permit the Spirit to fill us. The verb "fill" has nothing to do with contents or quantity, as though we are empty vessels that need a required amount of spiritual fuel to keep going. In the Bible, *filled* means "controlled by." "They... were filled with wrath" (Luke 4:28) means "they were controlled by wrath" and for that reason tried to kill Jesus. "The Jews were filled with envy" (Acts 13:45) means that the Jews were controlled by envy and opposed the ministry of Paul and Barnabas. To be "filled with the Spirit" means to be constantly controlled by the Spirit in our mind, emotions, and will...But how can a person tell whether or not he is filled with the Spirit? Paul stated that there are three evidences of

the fullness of the Spirit in the life of the believer: he is *joyful* (Eph. 5:19), *thankful* (Eph. 5:20), and *submissive* (Eph. 5:21–33). Paul said nothing about miracles or tongues, or other special manifestations.[5]

The Christian is commanded to be filled with the Spirit, but never forced. The filling of the Spirit is conditioned on the believer's willful surrender to do God's will. More so, the filling of the Spirit is an ongoing action in the life of the believer as he continually yields himself to God. The Christian must consciously live each moment of each day looking to God and thinking Scripture in every situation (Col. 3:1-3, 16; cf. Ps. 1:1-3). It is interesting to note that the filling of the Holy Spirit was often followed by divinely sanctioned speech (Luke 1:41-42; Acts 2:4; 4:8, 31; 13:8-10; Eph. 5:18-21). Lewis S. Chafer comments about the filling of the Spirit as follows:

> To be filled with the Spirit is to have the Spirit fulfilling in us all that God intended Him to do when he placed Him there. To be filled is not the problem of getting *more* of the Spirit: it is rather the problem of the Spirit getting *more* of us. We shall

---

[5] Warren Wiersbe, *The Bible Exposition Commentary: New Testament*, Vol. 2 (Colorado Springs, Col., Victor Books, 2001), 48.

never have *more* of the Spirit than the anointing which every true Christian has received. On the other hand, the Spirit may have all of the believer and thus be able to manifest in him the life and character of Christ. A spiritual person, then, is one who experiences the divine purpose and plan in his daily life through the power of the indwelling Spirit. The *character* of that life will be the out-lived Christ. The cause of that life will be the unhindered indwelling Spirit (Ephesians 3:16-21; 2 Corinthians 3:18).[6]

Once "filled with the Spirit" the believer is then to "walk by the Spirit" (Gal. 5:16). The word *walk* translates the Greek verb *peripateo* which carries the idea of continuous action. The verb is in the active voice which means the subject (i.e. the Christian) is to produce the action himself. The verb *walk* is preceded by the Greek noun *pneuma* (Spirit), which is in the dative case and expresses the idea of means; that is, he is to walk by means of the Holy Spirit. To put it simply, the Christian is to live his life in dependence on the Holy Spirit just as an elderly person may rely (or lean) on a cane or walker to move about.

---

[6] Lewis S. Chafer, *He that is Spiritual*, 43-44.

The New Testament calls the Christian life a "walk." This *walk* begins with a step of faith when we trust Christ as our Saviour. But salvation is not the end—it's only the beginning—of spiritual life. "Walking" involves progress, and Christians are supposed to advance in the spiritual life. Just as a child must learn to walk and must overcome many difficulties in doing so, a Christian must learn to "walk in the light."[7]

Being filled with the Spirit means the believer is allowing the Holy Spirit to guide his thoughts and actions. To walk in the Spirit means the believer is walking in moment by moment dependence on the Holy Spirit and living in accordance with God's Word. These truths are simple to understand, the challenge is in learning to execute them on regular basis rather than caving into the sinful pressures of the world.

---

[7] Warren Wiersbe, *The Bible Exposition Commentary: New Testament*, Vol. 2, 479.

Confess Your Sins

Indeed, there is not a righteous man on earth who *continually* does good and who never sins. (Eccl. 7:20)

If we confess our sins, He is faithful and righteous to forgive us our sins and to cleanse us from all unrighteousness. (1 John 1:9)

Once a person is *born again*, he is saved from the penalty of sin (Rom. 8:1; Eph. 2:5, 8), the power of sin (Rom. 6:11-14), and will ultimately be saved from the presence of sin when God takes him to heaven and gives him a new body like the body of Jesus (Phil. 3:20-21). Though Christians have a new nature in Christ (2 Cor. 5:17), they still possess a sinful nature and have the capacity to commit every sin possible (Rom. 7:19-21). Even the apostle Paul admitted that "evil is present in me, the one who wants to do good" (Rom. 7:21). When the Christian sins, he breaks fellowship with God, though he does not forfeit his salvation (1 John 1:3-10; cf. John 10:28).

During the commission of a sin, the Christian says "no" to the Holy Spirit and says "yes" either to the internal temptations of his sin nature or the external temptations of the world around him. As stated before, temptation is not sin, but the opportunity to sin. Sin can be either visible (words/actions) or invisible (mental) to others. The act of sin does not occur until the Christian yields to the temptation. A Christian may be tempted to lie, but he does not commit the sin of lying until he yields to the temptation and actually tells a lie. A Christian may be tempted to steal, but he does not commit the sin of stealing until he yields to the temptation and actually steals. At the very moment the sin is committed, fellowship with God is broken. The Christian is then under the control of his sin nature and is operating within Satan's world-system and remains there until that sin is confessed and fellowship with God is restored.

The word "confess" translates the Greek word *homologeo* which was a legal term used of a criminal who confessed his crime before a judge, admitting he was guilty of the accusation brought against him. When we sin, we are in violation of God's Word, and when we confess that sin, we are admitting that we are guilty as charged by God. To obtain forgiveness, we simply come to God and confess our sins by specifically naming them to Him. For example, we simply say to God "Father, I lied" or "Father, I lusted", and so on. God, who alone forgives the Christian's sin, requires nothing more than simple confession on the part of the believer and promises forgiveness every time (1 John 1:9).

God's forgiveness is never because the Christian feels sorry for his sin, or has paid penance, or done some other self justifying act. Forgiveness comes to the Christian because of the work of Christ who has born every sin on the cross. To ask the Christian to pay for his sin would be double jeopardy, because Christ has already paid the price for sin when he died on the cross. The Christian confesses his sin because he wants forgiveness and is seeking to restore fellowship with his heavenly Father. Regarding confession of sin, John F. Walvoord states:

> Complete assurance is given that this approach to the sin problem is acceptable to God. It is not a question of doing penance nor of inflicting chastening punishments upon oneself. Nor is it a matter of leniency with the Father when He accepts the confession. The whole act is based upon the finished work of Christ, and the question of penalty is not in view. The price for restoration has already

been paid. Accordingly, the Father is *faithful* and *righteous* in forgiving, not merely *lenient* and *merciful*. The Father could not do otherwise than forgive the Christian seeking forgiveness, for His own Son has already provided a complete satisfaction for sin. The process from the human side is, accordingly, amazingly simple.[8]

The believer, at any moment of his Christian life, is either carnal or spiritual. When carnal, the Christian's thoughts and actions are directed by his sin nature and he is out of fellowship with God. When spiritual, the Christian's thoughts and actions are directed by the Holy Spirit and he is in fellowship with God. Feelings have nothing to do either with carnality or spirituality. In fact, the Christian may feel great and be under the influence of his sin nature, or feel terrible and be under the direction of the Holy Spirit. Commission of sin gets the believer into a state of carnality and confession of sin restores fellowship with God.

When the believer is controlled by his sin nature his life will line up with world's value system and he will manifest the fruit of the flesh (Galatians 5:17-21). When

---

[8] John F. Walvoord, *The Holy Spirit*, 202.

the believer is controlled by the Holy Spirit his life will line up with the teaching of Scripture and he will manifest the fruit of the Spirit (Gal. 5:22-23). After the believer has learned to be filled with the Spirit and to walk in the Spirit, there is a need to grow daily through the intake and application of the Word of God.

> Therefore be careful how you walk, not as unwise men but as wise, making the most of your time, because the days are evil. So then do not be foolish, but understand what the will of the Lord is. (Eph. 5:15-17)

Time and testing are the final elements necessary to spiritual growth, as the Christian will not go from spiritual infancy to spiritual maturity without them. While in prison, the Christian must take advantage of the time afforded to him and study God's Word often and seek to make application whenever opportunity presents itself. He must make certain that he does not give in to the evil pressures of his environment, but stands for the Christian faith and lives for the will of God. As he grows spiritually, the following characteristics will manifest in his life and he will:

1. Submit to God's will (Jas. 4:7; cf. Rom. 12:1-2).

2. Seek to glorify God (1 Cor. 10:31).
3. Display a godly love (1 Cor. 13:4-8; 1 John 3:23).
4. Speak biblical truth (Eph. 4:15, 25).
5. Show humility (Eph. 4:1-2).
6. Be forgiving (Matt. 18:21-22).
7. Encourage others to do good works (Heb. 10:24).
8. Want to fellowship with Christians (Heb. 10:25).
9. Pray for others (2 Thess. 1:11).
10. Build others up in the Lord (1 Thess. 5:11).
11. Be devoted to fellow believers (Rom. 12:10).
12. Live by faith (Rom. 1:17).

God calls every Christian in prison to know and utilize the spiritual blessings He has given (Eph. 1:3). This requires study and a willingness to live a holy life in complete dependence on the Holy Spirit. As a result of living spiritually, Christian virtues such as love, grace, humility and kindness will shine forth like a bright light in a dark place. Where the light of Christianity shines, there a soul is free to live and love, even in the midst of spiritual darkness where evil forces rage. For all the inmates in prison who read this book, I pray with the apostle Paul:

That the God of our Lord Jesus Christ, the Father of glory, may give to you a spirit of wisdom and of revelation in the knowledge of Him. I pray that the eyes of your heart may be enlightened, so that you will know what is the hope of His calling, what are the riches of the glory of His inheritance in the saints, and what is the surpassing greatness of His power toward us who believe. (Eph. 1:17-19)

Chapter 7

Final Thoughts

These truths have been tested by many Christians since the church began nearly two thousand years ago and have been proven to sustain the believer in the harshest situations and bring glory to God. The prison environment sometimes provides a concentration of evil, but victory in the Christian life is not deterred because of that environment, since God and His Word are greater than anything Satan can create. Many people fall victim to the tyranny of inmates who are given over to evil and who perpetuate Satan's values in many of America's prisons. Yet, there are strong believers who have laid hold of God's Word and walked by means of the Spirit and proven to be a light in a dark place. Such men are heroes, having stood against the tide of evil that plagues our prisons today. God continues to look for good men, solid Christians, who will stand for truth and righteousness and show love to the unlovely and grace to the undeserving. We need more Christian heroes to take stand for Christ in America's jails and prisons and hopefully this book will provide some insight on how to accomplish that task. *Sola Gloria Dei – To God Alone is the Glory ~*

APPENDIX A

Biblical Hermeneutics
- Roy B. Zuck, *Basic Biblical Interpretation.*
- Bernard Ramm, *Protestant Biblical Interpretation.*
- Kaiser/Sylva, *Biblical Hermeneutics.*

Good Bible Translations
- *New American Standard Bible* (perhaps the best translation available).
- *New International Version* (good translation, but sometimes paraphrases).
- *Greek/English Interlinear Bible.*

Reference Books
- *Exhaustive Concordance of the Bible.*
- *The Treasury of Scripture Knowledge.*
- Carson/Moo, *An Introduction to the New Testament.*
- Gleason Archer, *A Survey of Old Testament Introduction.*
- *Vines Expository Dictionary of Old and New Testament Words.*
- Alfred Hoerth, *Archaeology & the Old Testament.*
- *The International Standard Bible Encyclopedia.*
- Merrill F. Unger, *Unger's Bible Dictionary.*

Theology
- Charles Ryrie, *Basic Theology.*
- Paul Enns, *Moody Handbook on Theology.*
- Chafer/Walvoord, *Major Bible Themes.*
- Lewis Chafer, *Eight Volume Systematic Theology* (for the advancing reader)

Commentaries
- Walvoord, Zuck, *The Bible Knowledge Commentary, Old Testament.*
- Walvoord, Zuck, *The Bible Knowledge Commentary, New Testament.*
- Warren Wiersbe, *The Bible Exposition Commentary* (six volumes for Old & New Testament).
- *Expositors Bible Commentary* (twelve volumes), (Frank Gaebelein chief editor)

Church History
- Philip Schaff, *History of the Christian Church.*
- John D. Hannah, *Our Legacy: History of Christian Doctrine.*

Prophecy
- Dwight Pentecost, *Things to Come.*
- Dwight Pentecost, *Prophecy for Today.*
- John F. Walvoord, *Major Bible Prophecies.*

Overcoming Evil in Prison

Overcoming Evil in Prison

BIBLIOGRAPHY

Bauer, Walter. *A Greek-English Lexicon of the New Testament and Other Early Christian Literature*, 3rd ed. Revised and edited by Fredrick William Danker. Chicago: University of Chicago Press, 2000.

Brown, Francis, Driver, S.R. and Briggs, Charles A. *The New Brown-Driver-Briggs-Gesenius Hebrew-English Lexicon*. Peabody, Mass.: Hendrickson Publishers 1979.

Bromily, Geoffrey W. *International Standard Bible Encyclopedia*, 4 Vols. Michigan: Eerdmans Publishing Company, 1986.

Chafer, Lewis S. "Revelation" *Bibliotheca Sacra* 94 (1937): 265-281.

Chafer, Lewis S. *He that is Spiritual*. Grand Rapids: Zondervan Publishing, 1967.

Chafer, Lewis S. *The Epistle to the Ephesians*. Grand Rapids: Kregel Publications, 1991.

Cooper, David L. *The God of Israel*. Los Angeles: Biblical Research Society, 1945.

Enns, Paul. *The Moody Handbook of Theology*. Chicago: Moody Press, 1997.

Fruchtenbaum, Arnold G. *The Book of Genesis: Exposition from a Messianic Jewish Perspective.* San Antonio, TX. Ariel Ministries, 2009.

Karleen, Paul S. *The Handbook to Bible Study: With a Guide to the Scofield Study System.* New York: Oxford University Press, 1987.

Lightner, Robert P. *Handbook of Evangelical Theology.* Grand Rapids: Kregel Publications, 1995.

Lightner, Robert P. *Safe in the Arms of Jesus.* Grand Rapids: Kregel Publications, 2000.

Lloyd-Jones, David Martyn. *The Church and the Last Things.* Wheaton, Ill.: Crossway Books, 1998.

Morris, Henry M., *The Genesis Record: A Scientific and Devotional Commentary on the Book of Beginnings.* Grand Rapids: Baker Books, 1976.

New American Standard Bible Updated © 1995 by The Lockman Foundation.

Ryrie, Charles C. *A Survey of Bible Doctrine.* Chicago: Moody Press, Chicago: Moody Press, 1995.

Unger, Merrill F. *The New Unger's Bible Dictionary*. Chicago: Moody Press, 1988.

Walvoord, John F. *The Holy Spirit*. Grand Rapids: Zondervan Publishing, 1977.

Wiersbe, Warren. *The Bible Exposition Commentary, 6 Volumes*. Wheaton: Victor Books, 2001.

Workman, Herbert B. *Persecution in the Early Church*. Cincinnati: Jennings & Graham, 1906.

Zuck, Roy B. "The Work of the Holy Spirit in Illumination" *Bibliotheca Sacra* 141 (1984): 121-131.

Overcoming Evil in Prison

Overcoming Evil in Prison

Made in the USA
Lexington, KY
21 June 2012